Praise for
Emotionally Healthy Twins:

"Finally . . . a definitive guide—from someone who understands both professionally and personally—to raising twins as individuals. A must-read for parents of multiples!"

—ELIZABETH LYONS, AUTHOR OF *READY OR NOT . . . THERE WE GO!*
THE REAL EXPERTS' GUIDE TO THE TODDLER YEARS WITH TWINS

"As the mother of twins, I highly recommend Dr. Friedman's book. If only I had this resource when our little ones were babies. Emotionally Healthy Twins *shows parents how to get over the 'twin mystique' and help their children know the freedom of just being themselves."*

—LYN DAVIS LEAR, PH.D., COFOUNDER AND MEMBER OF THE
BOARD OF THE ENVIRONMENTAL MEDIA ASSOCIATION,
WIFE OF PRODUCER AND PHILANTHROPIST NORMAN LEAR

"Parents of twins are starving for useful information about raising well-adjusted twins; the need to have a comprehensive book of raising twins is tremendous. Well-written, full of innovative and helpful advice, and fun to read, Dr. Friedman's book should be a part of any parent's repertoire on raising healthy twins. Dr. Friedman's parenting-of-twins philosophy is sensible and enjoyable. The advice given in this book is not only useful in raising well-adjusted twins, but also pertinent to raising children in general. I highly recommend this book to all parents of twins."

—SHERYL A. ROSS, M.D., CONTRIBUTOR,
TWO AT A TIME: HAVING TWINS AND
MEDICAL EXPERT, *EXPECTING FITNESS*

"As a principal faced with an increasing number of twins at school, I welcome Dr. Friedman's book. Parents of twins have preconceived ideas as to what schooling should be like for their children. Key among their fears is separation of twins into different rooms. Likewise, school systems can be intransigent in their policies concerning placement of twins. Dr. Friedman considers these issues from many sides and offers ample evidence of things to consider about the development of twins. It will help parents make schooling for their twins more productive and appropriate."

—MARGARITA M. MUÀIZ, PRINCIPAL,
RAFAEL HERNANDEZ SCHOOL

"Combining her knowledge as a psychotherapist with her personal experience, both as a twin and as a parent of twins, Dr. Joan Friedman offers a practical, innovative approach to raising well-adjusted twins."

—JEFFREY WASSON, M.D., PEDIATRICIAN

Emotionally Healthy

twins

Emotionally Healthy

twins

. . . .

A New Philosophy
for Parenting Two
Unique Children

JOAN A. FRIEDMAN, PH.D.

Da Capo
LIFE
LONG

A Member of the Perseus Books Group

Designed by Pauline Brown
Set in 16-point Palatino by the Perseus Books Group

Library of Congress Cataloging-in-Publication Data

Friedman, Joan A.
    Emotionally healthy twins : a new philosophy for parenting two unique children /
Joan A. Friedman. — 1st Da Capo Press ed.
        p. cm. — (Lifelong books)
    Includes index.
    ISBN-13: 978-0-7382-1087-2 (pbk. : alk. paper)
    ISBN-10: 0-7382-1087-0 (pbk. : alk. paper) 1. Twins—Care. 2. Twins—Psychology.
3. Parent and child. 4. Parenting. I. Title.
    HQ777.35.F73 2007
    649'.144--dc22

                                                                    2007030330

Published by Da Capo Press
A Member of the Perseus Books Group
www.dacapopress.com

NOTE: The information in this book is true and complete to the best of our knowledge. This book is intended only as an informative guide for those wishing to know more about health issues. In no way is this book intended to replace, countermand, or conflict with the advice given to you by your own physician. The ultimate decision concerning care should be made between you and your doctor. We strongly recommend you follow his or her advice. Information in this book is general and is offered with no guarantees on the part of the authors or Da Capo Press. The authors and publisher disclaim all liability in connection with the use of this book. The names and identifying details of people associated with events described in this book have been changed. Any similarity to actual persons is coincidental.

10 9 8 7 6 5 4 3 2 1

To my husband, Robert, and my children,
Matthew, Sarah, Amy, Jonny, and David

Contents

• one •

TWO UNIQUE
CHILDREN

I was thrilled to find out I was pregnant with twin boys. My family would have the chance to welcome two babies into the world and to delight in watching them grow. And I would have the chance to revisit the world of twins from a new perspective. Would my sons have as much fun growing up together as my identical twin sister, Jane, and I had? I remembered our closeness and the many happy times we had shared. But I also remembered how being a twin had often been an obstacle for me and how I had struggled to sort out my twin issues as an adult. So, along with my excitement about becoming the mother of twins, I faced a challenge. I wanted each boy to take pleasure in his relationship with his twin brother but also to discover and appreciate his own uniqueness.

I began to consider how I might raise my sons so that they would enjoy many of the positive experiences that Jane and I had as twins, without the twinship difficulties we endured simply because we were twins. Jane and I loved each other from a place no one else could fully understand. We were always there for each other and still are. Yet, as a child and a teenager, I sometimes resented not being known for myself but, rather, as half of the twins Joan and Jane. From a young age, I suffered because I felt it was my responsibility as Jane's twin to make sure she was happy and comfortable. Worrying that my actions, and even my feelings, might make her unhappy depleted my energy and held me back from discovering who I was. I often felt sad because it was so hard to be an authentic, separate person who could do, say, and be whatever I wanted without feeling pressured to consider the effects on Jane.

Jane never asked me to behave this way; nor was she aware that I often felt sad, pressured, or resentful. But the powerful twin dynamic that developed between us became the most important influence on my emotional life. So, when I learned that I was about to become the mother of twins, I knew I needed to practice the parenting-of-twins philosophy that I had developed from my history as a twin and as a psychotherapist specializing in the treatment of twins and their parents. For years I had helped parents in my parents-of-twins support groups and workshops, as well as in individual sessions, to deal with the issues that arise in the raising of twins. I had also counseled twins, both children and adults, who were struggling with identity issues. Now it was time for me to put my professional wisdom to the test in a more personal way.

The core tenet of my philosophy is that parents and others need to treat twins as two separate children who happen to have been born at the same time. This perspective goes far beyond the conventional advice to dress twins differently and choose names that don't begin with the same letter of the alphabet. Authentically perceiving and treating twins as two unique children may involve fundamentally changing your mind about what it means to be a twin, adjusting your expectations abou[...] should interact, and even giving up some of the alleged "benefits" of having two children who are the same age.

Throughout this book, we will explore how to practice this parenting-of-twins philosophy at every stage of your twins' lives, from preinfancy to young adulthood, with the goal of ensuring that they have the same opportunities to develop their individual selves as do children born individually ("singletons," as I'll refer to them).

My twin sons, Jonny and David, are now eighteen. Each is proud of his strengths and abilities, and neither feels the need to hide his successes for fear he might hurt his brother's self-esteem. The two are close friends but have not been overly dependent on each other. Of course, like most siblings, they are competitive at times, but because my husband, Robert, and I have focused on each boy's uniqueness and given both opportunities to develop as individuals, neither defines himself by how he compares to his twin brother.

Throughout Jonny and David's lives, my husband and I have understood that our job as parents is to help each child grow and develop as a unique individual. From day one, we made sure that the boys enjoyed one-on-one time with each of us, that they experienced themselves as distinct children, and that they enjoyed separate experiences that would help them define who they are and who they want to become.

Each of these strategies falls into the parenting-of-twins philosophy that you'll learn more about in this chapter. It is my hope that, by understanding the philosophy and employing such strategies in the raising of your twins, no matter how old they are, you, as parents, your twins, and their siblings will reap the joys of twinship and successfully manage the challenges that this special sibling relationship brings.

The Twin Mystique

As we begin to consider a new perspective on how to raise emotionally healthy twins, it's important to think about how twins are romanticized in our culture. Stereotypically, most people think of twins as intensely close soul mates connected to each other through a kind of sibling ESP. Many of us assume that one twin not only knows what the other is thinking and feeling but can automatically provide what the other needs. Twins are seen as inhabiting their own private world for which only they hold the map. It is assumed that each feels lost without the other and that they seek to preserve their twosome status even as adults. Non-twins fantasize that, in a twin relationship, one always knows what the other one wants and needs, and for this reason, it is thought that twins are each other's predestined partner and confidant.

Each of these assumptions contributes to what I call the "twin mystique," a mystique that has been around for a very long time. So, why do so many people cling to the mystique? What's behind the infatuation with twins as mysterious, inseparable, and magical? There is something inherently captivating about the idea of having a double because it invokes a human longing for an intimate, lifelong companion who thoroughly understands us. With such a companion, we feel we would never be abandoned or alone. People project this longing onto twins and see them as enjoying an idealized relationship.

In fact, twins can be lifelong friends, and they can fulfill many emotional needs for each other. But if they are expected to fulfill the fantasy of telepathic soul mates who inhabit a mysteriously wonderful world of their own, they will not feel free to develop on their own. When the longing to see twins in a romanticized way prevents parents and others from seeing them as individuals, twins feel as if they are merely playing a role in someone else's fantasy.

And then there are the cultural references that further embellish the romantic notion of hyperconnected, indivisible twins. Media images portray twins as cute, funny, mischievous, and seductive, and, again, as sharing a unique telepathic bond. The long-lost twins in *The Parent Trap*, the adorable-turned-foxy Olsen twins, the wholesomely seductive Doublemint gum twins who promise to double your pleasure and your fun: each of these pairs feeds our fantasies about what it would be like to double our enjoyment of life by being a twin or simply hanging out with twins. The myth of inseparableness is perpetuated by such diverse cultural icons as Tweedledum and Tweedledee in *Through the Looking Glass and What Alice Found There* (*Alice in Wonderland*); Marge's cynical, chain-smoking twin sisters, Patty and Selma, on TV's *The Simpsons;* and the squeaky-clean Bobbsey twins in the classic children's book series.

Although the equally rotund Tweedledum and Tweedledee express contrary opinions, they appear to Alice as inseparably joined, each one's arm firmly encircling the other's neck. In fact, Alice perceives them as so closely connected that she becomes anxious about whose hand to shake first, fearing she'll hurt the other's feelings. To resolve the dilemma, she shakes both their hands at the same time!

Marge Simpson's twin sisters, Patty and Selma, have indistinguishable gravelly voices and display the exact same crankiness. Their sisterly bond extends to the fact that, although now middle-aged, they still live together and never go anywhere without each other.

The Bobbsey twins are actually two sets of twins from the same family—the older twins, Nan and Bert, and the younger, blonder twins, Flossie and Freddie. In the book series, which has appealed to young readers for more than a hundred years, theirs is an idealized, happy family in which neither set of twins ever has any interpersonal conflicts. Both sets of twins are adventurous duos, and it's clear that their adventures could never take place if they weren't always together.

Sometimes it is twins themselves who contribute to the twin mystique. They may exploit their twinship in order to attract attention—or customers. For instance, a restaurant in New York City is owned by twin sisters and staffed by thirty-seven sets of identical twins, with each set working the same shift. *New York Times* restaurant critic Ruth Reichl became an inadvertent cheerleader for the twin mystique with this cleverly written restaurant review: "Twins sounds like a pretty silly gimmick. Until you get there. When you are greeted at the door by two gorgeous and identical hostesses, then glance at the bar to find two identical men pouring drinks, the idea begins to grow on you. By the time a pair of waitresses arrives, one wearing a sign saying 'I'm not Lisa,' the other a sign saying 'I'm not Debbie,' it is hard not to be charmed. Twins, owned by one pair of twins and staffed by many others, creates its own giddy world of doubles. Most times there are twins at some of the tables as well, which makes those of us who came into the world alone feel as if we were somehow cheated. Where are our doubles?"[1] Reichl adds that a pack of Doublemint gum comes with the check.

It seems everyone wants to buy into the twin mystique. Twinsburg, Ohio, has put itself on the map by hosting an annual "Twins Days Festival," drawing more than three thousand sets of twins from across the country who compete in talent shows, as well as for titles proclaiming "most alike" and "least alike." In response to a frequently asked question on their Web site, "Do we have to dress alike?" festival organizers respond that, although some twins hate calling attention to themselves by dressing alike in "real life," at the festival you stand out by dressing differently: "It's part of the festival to dress up. Heck, there are even boy/girl twins who dress alike, just to show their common bond to any doubters who might say, 'Hey, you're not a twin!' Many sets don't normally dress alike. Some, though, enjoy dressing alike whenever they go out together. More power to 'em, I say. Wish I had that kinda confidence to stand out in public." The message seems to be, the more bonded to your twin and the more confident you are as a person, the more you'll want to dress like a twin forever.

At a recent Twins Days Festival, the Discovery Health Channel scouted for "America's Most Identical Twins." The festival organizers identified sets of twins who shared similar personality traits, as well as food and fashion preferences. Those judged to be the most alike later underwent a battery of tests and were filmed separately while ordering in a restaurant, shopping for an outfit,

1. Ruth Reichl, "Twins at Twins—Diner's Journal," *New York Times*, January 13, 1995.

and meeting a prospective dating partner. But guess what happened? The twin brothers who were found to be the most identical according to the Discovery Channel's psychological and behavioral criteria reported that they actually felt quite different from one another and were thus surprised by the findings. They believed that they were different, even if the show organizers, judges, and television audience perceived them as behaving identically.[2]

Why the ongoing focus on behavioral similarities in twins? Although many psychological studies emphasize the individuality of twins and the latest scientific research reveals that even identical twins are different on a cellular level, the general public still has the desire to find twins to be more similar than they actually are. Again, there is a longing for twinship to be about like-mindedness, which seems to have been behind the Discovery Channel's attempt to prove how alike twins are behaviorally.

Twins used to be relatively rare, contributing to society's fascination with them. With the prevalence of infertility treatments, which increase the number of fertilized eggs, twins have become increasingly common. Between 1994 and 2004, the multiple-birth ratio in the United States increased 32 percent. In our country in 2004, 3.4 percent of live births were multiple deliveries,[3] marking a dramatic increase in the number of twins. Despite a concurrent increase in scientific research related to twins, the twin mystique persists, and fantasies about twinship still dominate.

A New Parenting-of-Twins Philosophy

While many parents of twins seem to embrace the concept of encouraging individuality, most unwittingly undermine it. Getting

2. Nancy L. Segal, "More Extraordinary Lives of Twins," *Twin Research and Human Genetics* (June 2006): 477.

3. National Center for Health Statistics, *Final Natality Data*, March of Dimes, 2007, available at www.marchofdimes.com/peristats (accessed May 15, 2007).

caught up in the twin mystique is hard to avoid when relatives, friends, and the media persist in promoting it. But when you consider how crucial it is for each of your children to develop a unique sense of themselves and the freedom to decide who they want to become without being typecast as half of a twin set, your parenting decisions will be that much easier. The following are my core parenting guidelines for helping your twins develop into happy, self-realized, unique individuals. In the chapters to come, we'll see how each of these concepts can be applied to the parenting of twins at every stage of their development.

1. Think of your twins as two unique individuals.

Twins need to be addressed as individual children who will grow up to be individual adults. If you relate to them as "twins" rather than as separate beings, they will relate to each other and the world as "twins" because that will be the reality they'll know. Thinking of your children as distinct individuals from the moment you are told you're pregnant with twins will ensure that they think of themselves as unique.

This concept may seem obvious, but every parenting decision you make will be based on it. If you think of your children as two separate individuals, rather than as "the twins," your treatment of them will follow accordingly. It's a question of creating a new mind-set. It may help to remind yourself repeatedly that twins are two babies who happen to have been born at the same time, not conjoined souls destined to be forever linked together.

2. Expect to have different feelings for each child.

Even parents of singletons can feel guilty about having different feelings for each of their children. Parents of twins tend to feel such guilt even more strongly. If you accept that your children are unique, however, it only makes sense that they will elicit different feelings in you. Feeling impatient with one twin baby and delighted by the other, feeling angry at one two-year-old's willfulness and relieved that the other plays happily by herself, or even feeling that you have more in common with one preteen twin than the other does not mean that you love one child more than the other. Accepting that you have different feelings in response to your children's behavior and personalities means that you acknowledge their uniqueness.

I have read many studies of twins, each of which lists various reasons why parents may prefer one baby over the other. For example, one study shows that when babies don't come home from the hospital at the same time due to medical reasons, the baby who comes home first may be preferred because the second baby is perceived as an intruder. Other studies reveal that some parents prefer the smaller twin, the more sociable twin, the twin who sleeps longer, the twin who cries less. The important thing to remember is not to suppress your feelings; they are normal and to be expected. Suppressing how you feel can result in unnecessary guilt and uncertainty about your parenting abilities. In fact, preferring one child to the other for such reasons as those listed above changes with time because children's behavior constantly shifts, and so do your reactions to it. Being conscious of your distinct emotional responses to each child and accepting those distinctions will help you normalize feelings that are simply a fact of life in raising twins.

3. Give each child consistent "alone time" with you. They need it in order to adequately bond with you.

Every infant benefits from one-on-one time with his or her parent; it helps fulfill a basic human need. If a newborn could talk, he would likely say, "Pay attention to me, look at me, listen to me, know me." A child and his or her parent will know each other better with the opportunity for regular, focused time together. Tuning in to your child's needs in the first year of life helps you attune to your baby's emotional and physical communications, and this attunement is enhanced when you are with one baby at a time. As your baby experiences your responses to him again and again, a secure attachment develops. He comes to expect that he will be appropriately soothed when he is hungry or tired, happy or excited. Allowing him to get to know you—and feel known by you—helps lay the foundation for his sense of who he is in relationship to the world.

The importance of alone time with one's parent doesn't end at infancy. It extends throughout one's entire childhood.

4. Don't attempt to provide a "fair and equal" child-hood for your twins.

Just as it is impossible to create a completely safe environment for our children, it is also impossible to create a fair and equal one. Yet most parents, especially parents of twins, understandably feel the need to do just that. In fact, an important part of our job is to help our children learn how to adapt to or overcome unfair circumstances. If we're always trying to make things "fair" for them, they might not learn how to meet this challenge. Learning to cope with unfairness and inequality is an inescapable emotional task. As parents, when we attempt to create a fair and equal environment for our twins, however well meaning we might be, we give them a false impression about themselves and the world and inhibit their ability to deal with life's inevitable inequalities. Life is not fair, and twins are not equal.

As a twin and a mother of twins, the notion of inequality is something I have always treasured because it denotes distinctions between two separate people. When you treat each twin differently, you communicate to your children that you realize they are distinct individuals. And as parents, we can redefine "fair" to mean fair with regard to each child's unique needs and emotional makeup.

5. Don't compare twins to each other; each is on his or her unique life path.

Twins begin life in the same place at the same time, but that doesn't mean they are headed in the same direction.

Too often, parents believe they are helping their twins by making distinctions based on how each compares to the other. While saying, "He's the athletic one, unlike his brother, the math whiz," may sound benign, all children want to be seen in their own light, not in the shadow of someone else. Even siblings who are not twins don't like to be compared to each other. They need their parents to know who they really are, not how they stack up against their brother or sister. For twins, this need is especially strong.

Labeling one twin with one description and the other twin with another is usually a well-meaning attempt by parents to differentiate between their two children—Linda is the creative one; Laura is the scholar. Unfortunately, the labels can stick. When used frequently, they affect how others see the twins and how the twins see themselves. So, the label becomes a limiting, self-fulfilling prophecy. As parents of twins, we need to make a special effort not to promote comparisons and labels to define our children. We must respect that children constantly change and develop in their unique ways. Helping them gain the tools they'll need to chart their own paths is much more beneficial to their personal growth than saddling them with restrictive labels.

6. Encourage twins to pursue their own friendships and interests.

Being the same age and most often going to the same schools, twins draw from the same pool of potential friends. But it is important that each child be encouraged to develop her own friendships, apart from her twin. Again, this is part of the individuation process through which children come to develop a distinct self, personally and socially. Engaging in activities that reflect their own interests and having experiences separate from their twin likewise helps children and teens to discover and define themselves as individuals.

As parents of twins, part of our job is to ensure that each child has sufficient opportunities to seek out his own friends and develop his own interests, apart from his twin sibling. We need to create these opportunities for our children beginning when they are very young, and we can only do so if we accept how important separate experiences are for each child's individual growth.

7. Don't rely on your twins to be each other's constant companion or surrogate parent.

With today's hectic schedules, it can be a relief for parents to assume that their twins seem naturally to want to be together and to take care of each other. As young children, they may seem like built-in playmates; as they get older, they may appear to enjoy being each other's best friend and most trusted confidant. And one twin may actually take on the role of surrogate parent, seeing to the other's emotional needs. But when "too much togetherness" shuts out parents and others, twins don't learn to socialize in an age-appropriate manner. And the lack of psychological boundaries between twin children can lead to confused roles and, sometimes, inappropriate behavior.

One of the dangers of twins parenting each other is that they develop an intense need to maintain an emotional equilibrium. This means that in order not to rock the boat of their overly close connection, each child denies her own feelings or prevents herself from branching out on her own for fear of upsetting the other. When twins become each other's parental figure, it may be a sign that their actual parents are not adequately fulfilling their parental roles. All children, even those who have close relationships with a sibling, need focused attention, guidance, and emotional support from their parents. Twins shouldn't be expected to provide these for each other.

An Invitation

Raising emotionally healthy twins is more involved than simply memorizing these seven points and vowing to adhere to them. In the upcoming chapters, as you read about how other parents have successfully used the seven-point philosophy to face the unique challenges of parenting their twins, I hope you will be inspired and encouraged. Whether you've just found out you're pregnant with twins or are the parent of twin teens, I invite you to consider your own emerging twin-parenting story as you hear about how others have shaped theirs.

As to how this twin-parenting philosophy relates to identical versus fraternal twins, the issues are quite similar. While parents of identical twins must be even more aware of the need to perceive and treat each child as a unique individual, parents of fraternal twins also need to adhere closely to the seven principles.

Whether twins are identical or fraternal, they must be valued for their individuality, and they need their parents to teach them to develop their unique abilities, as well as to handle the inevitable competition and comparison with their same-age sibling. It's true that these challenges can be greater for identical twins and for fraternal twins of the same sex, but regardless of which type of twins yours are, the seven principles will guide you in making sure that your same-age children have every opportunity to grow into the emotionally healthy, self-determined individuals they deserve to be.

· two ·
MENTALLY PREPARING FOR TWO SEPARATE BABIES

Once we got the news that I was having twins, my husband and I couldn't stop talking about the twins this and the twins that. Every mental image I had of them was of . . . them! Together. Together in their stroller, playing together in their playpen, sleep mates keeping each other company in their crib. When I joined the parents-of-twins group and started talking to others about what to expect, I realized that I hadn't really stopped to think of each baby apart from the other. That was quite a revelation.

—CRYSTAL, MOTHER OF TWINS

Relating to your twins as separate individuals begins the moment you find out you're pregnant with two babies. Like Crystal and many other expectant parents of twins, you may find that the phrase "I'm pregnant with two babies" sounds a bit strange. But referring to your future children in this way actually makes a difference in how you think about them, and it's never too early to begin connecting with each child as one of a kind rather than as half of a duo. In fact, as you plan for your babies' arrival, it is important to consider each of the seven points discussed in the last chapter and to think about how you might incorporate them into your future role as the parent of twins. Knowing that your attitude in approaching each twin is vital to his or her healthy development will inspire you to try the strategies I'll be suggesting in this chapter, some of which may strike you as quite unusual.

To begin with, why not welcome each baby-to-be with a private conversation? Communicating with each twin is a way to begin the bonding process, as well as thinking of each baby as separate from the other. During pregnancy, you can send the message to each baby—however you choose to do so—that you are looking forward to his or her arrival as a uniquely cherished individual. Whether you talk or sing to each child or simply communicate silently with each one, it is important to acknowledge that in your mind and in your heart you perceive each baby as distinct and special. If you begin sending this message while your babies are still growing inside you (or your partner), welcoming each one into the world as a separate person will feel that much more natural.

Each of us needs to feel unique and adequate in our own right. If, in the mind of her parent, a child's identity is primarily defined by her being a twin, it becomes very difficult for her to reach her potential as an individual human being. Throughout this chapter, we'll hear from expectant parents who began preparing for their two babies by employing strategies to help them think about each twin as an individual. And I'll help you consider the issues that arise during pregnancy that relate to perceiving your twins as two separate babies.

In case you're wondering whether this individuality thing is solely a psychological matter, consider what scientists have to say about the biological individuality of twins.

Two Biologically Unique Babies

As expectant parents of twins who are learning to relate to your babies as individuals, it will help you to know that several scientific studies support the biological individuality of twins. In fact, research shows that even identical twins are not actually identical. While identical twins share the exact same DNA, studies reveal that they do not have an identical epigenetic profile, meaning that there are differences in identical twins' cellular development. Indeed, scientists are finding that the cellular makeup of identical twins differentiates as they age. And environmental influences, such as dietary habits and living conditions, also impact each twin's cellular organization. Future studies may help explain how differences in cellular organization result in one identical twin's suffering from a particular condition while the other one does not.[1]

Researchers are finding other differences between identical twins as well. Neuropsychiatrist and psychoanalyst Alessandra Piontelli writes that, in twin pregnancies, no two fetuses have the exact same intrauterine conditions. You may notice, for example, that when observing your twins on ultrasounds, one may be poking the other, one may be taking up more space, or one may

1. Nicholas Wade, "Explaining Differences in Twins," *New York Times*, July 5, 2005, available at www.nytimes.com (accessed September 13, 2005).

appear to be much more active than the other. Since no two fetuses have identical environments in which to develop, each fetus's interaction with its environment, including nutritional intake, is at least slightly different, which in turn produces physical and behavioral differences. Piontelli also reports that the distinct personalities of each fetus highlighted in ultrasounds further debunks the myth of identicalness. "Ultrasounds allow us to catch a glimpse of the dawning of individual dispositions," she observes. "Recognising [sic] that the intrauterine environment is not neutral, but favors and shapes individual differences, may further encourage us to look at so-called identical twins as behaviorally distinct and unique human beings from the start."[2]

Since this fascinating research concludes that individuality in twins is a biological fact, we can feel even more confident as parents that we're doing the right thing by emphasizing each child's individuality, even at this prebirth phase of development.

A Note of Caution

A lot of parents who have watched their twins on a sonogram talk about differences they perceived in fetal behavior and how this seemed to determine the babies' behavior once they were born. Perhaps one fetus kicked the other, or one seemed to stifle the other by taking up more room in the womb. Such observations often lead parents to attribute permanent qualities to their twin children. For example, one of my clients talked about how one of her twins had had more problems because "he was squished by his twin in the womb." I understand that parents characterize

---

2. Alessandra Piontelli, *Twins: From Fetus to Child* (London: Routledge, 2002), 43.

their children in this way in order to try to differentiate who the babies are and who they will become. But such prenatal labeling as "he's the pushy one; she's the passive one" attributes qualities to children that may not be correct or real in any way. Just because a fetus seems to be cramped and less active on the sonogram doesn't mean she'll grow up to be passive. But sometimes well-meaning parents of twins will see a behavior after birth and say, "Oh, of course he acts that way; he was on top of his brother in utero for nine months!"

The twin mystique is largely responsible for such unrealistic generalizations because it involves attributing a child's behavior to the particular relationship he has to his twin. How one fetus appeared to relate to the other in the womb becomes a way of describing a baby's, toddler's, or teenager's personality, with little focus on more meaningful ways of understanding each individual twin or how they relate with one another.

Remember, not only are your babies unique individuals, but they are defined by many more influences than simply their relationship to each other—inside or outside of the womb. And in the first stages of life, the parent-child relationship, not the intrauterine communication between twins, is the most important aspect of a child's development.

Mixed Emotions

Before we explore a new way to announce to others that you're pregnant with twins, it's important for you to acknowledge your own emotional response to the news. Finding out that you're having twins can elicit a myriad of emotions, some of which expectant parents of twins often feel guilty about or ashamed of. Even if you had anticipated the possibility of twins due to in vitro procedures or genetic history, learning for certain that you'll be bringing two babies into the world at the same time is an emotional jolt.

According to Linda G. Leonard of the Multiple Births Support Program at the University of British Columbia's School of Nursing and Jane Denton of the Multiple Births Foundation at Queen Charlotte's and Chelsea Hospital in London in a paper entitled "Preparation for Parenting Multiple Birth Children," parents' responses to the news that they're expecting more than one baby can include a combination of shock, ambivalence, anxiety, and distress—as well as pride, elation, and fulfillment. Unlike parents who learn they are expecting one baby and generally feel both elated and anxious, parents who find out they are expecting two feel those things and a whole lot more.

The women in my mothers-of-twins groups openly reveal their mix of positive and not-so-positive emotions. If they are first-time parents-to-be and have struggled to get pregnant or undergone months, even years, of in vitro treatments, their initial reactions are, of course, elation and triumph. Women feel they finally belong; they are at last entitled to join the most primal of sororities: birth mothers. Men who have experienced with their wives the possibility of permanent infertility may feel especially validated and proud about having twins. After trying, failing, and trying again and again to help create a baby, they are now thrilled to be expecting two. If you and your partner went through in vitro and are now pregnant with twins, chances are you use words like "grateful," "blessing," "ecstatic," and even "miracle" to describe how you both feel about the happy news.

Even expectant parents who have not undergone in vitro are generally delighted with the news that they'll be having twins. Two babies at once are a very special, joy-filled bundle and definitely cause for a double celebration.

But then, there are the less-than-joyful, yet very common, emotional responses, many of which parents expecting twins tend to keep under wraps. First, there is the shock. Contemplating the reality of two babies instead of one—being pregnant with them, delivering them, and somehow managing to care for them—is enough to send anyone into a panic. Parents worry that they won't be able to handle the sheer physical work of taking care of two babies at once, that they won't be able to give each one adequate attention or be able to cope financially. If they already have children, they worry about devoting enough time to them once the twins arrive. Women who work outside the home may fear a loss of identity due to the need to cut back on working hours or put their career on hold. Parents expecting twins are also understandably concerned about the increased physical risks for the babies, as well as maternal hardships during pregnancy, including a higher incidence of low birth weight, prematurity, a greater risk of cerebral palsy, less physical activity for the mother-to-be, and a greater possibility that she will require bed rest during her pregnancy. For all of these emotional and physical reasons, expectant parents of twins may secretly wish they were having only one baby and feel terribly guilty for harboring such thoughts.

Tori came to see me because she couldn't express her conflicted feelings to either her husband or her friends. This is what she shared with me:

> *After years of trying to get pregnant and then finally receiving the news that I was having twins, I was delirious with joy—at least for the first few days. Then the anxiety set in. How am I ever going to handle this? Two babies at the same time—am I crazy? I can barely handle babysitting my niece and nephew for an entire evening—and they're grown-up kids of five and seven! I remember how jealous I was of my sister's pregnancies, and now I feel jealous that she got to have one baby at a time. I hate myself for being jealous—shouldn't I just be grateful for getting what I've wanted for so long?*

Like Tori, you may feel that being grateful for finally getting pregnant precludes acknowledging your fears about what lies ahead, and like her, you may feel guilty when you do. On the other hand, if you had a hard time getting pregnant, you may be less inclined to face some of the more negative emotions and daunting realities associated with having twins.

Even if you conceived naturally, if the twins are your first children, you may simply be unaware of what parenting entails and thus not acknowledge the difficulties you will likely encounter having two babies at once. Joyful anticipation may be all you're feeling at the moment, and I certainly encourage you to treasure that. But it's also important to prepare yourself mentally for the challenging realities of being a parent to two babies at the same time so that you won't be as overwhelmed once they arrive.

If you are already the parent of one or more singletons, you may underestimate what is involved in parenting two babies. Being the mother or father of twins doesn't equate to simply the singleton experience times two. Parents who receive the twins news with an overconfident "I've done it before; I can do it again" may be in for a double whammy down the line. Not only will they be shocked by how different parenting twins is, but they may be terribly disappointed that the experience isn't the same as caring for a single baby.

When you take the time to find out as much as you can about what parenting twins realistically involves—and reading this book is a good start—you will help prevent the possibility of postdelivery exhaustion, disappointment, and despair. The more realistic you are about what to expect from the parenting-of-twins experience, the more likely you are to enjoy the rich and delightful—yet challenging, exhausting, and overwhelming— experience of being the mother or father of two babies.

Whatever your feelings upon hearing that twins are on the way, it is crucial that you own up to them. Suppressing your emotions will only make you feel more distressed and postpone the inevitability of dealing with them. Share what you're feeling with someone you trust who will show compassion about what you're going through. Hopefully, you can level with your spouse about the mixed emotions brought on by the twins news. I also highly recommend joining a support group for parents expecting twins. Sharing with and learning from each other and a facilita-tor, such as a psychotherapist familiar with twin issues, will diffuse the sense of panic and help you deal with your conflicted emotions.

Announcing the Good News

Thinking of your two babies-to-be as separate beings is vital in raising them to become healthy individuals, and how you refer to them even before they're born makes a difference in solidifying this mind-set. So how do you make the pregnancy announcement in a way that will strengthen your resolve to have others think of your babies in the same, separate way that you are now thinking of them?

It may seem unfamiliar to announce to your friends and family, "We're having two babies!" rather than, "We're having twins!" but when you state the news in this way, you'll be laying the foundation for how you, your friends, and your family relate to your children. So here's a hypothetical scenario. See if you can imagine yourself in the role of parent-to-be:

PARENT-TO-BE: I have some wonderful news! Brad and I are going to be the parents of two babies!

MOTHER-IN-LAW: What do you mean? Are you saying you're having twins?

PARENT-TO-BE: Yes, but we're already thinking about them as two separate children because that is what they are: two separate babies born at the same time.

MOTHER-IN-LAW: What's wrong with calling them twins?

PARENT-TO-BE: Nothing's wrong with it. It's just that Brad and I feel strongly about relating to our babies as two

distinct children rather than as a pair. And we hope that
our friends and family will treat them as individuals as well.
MOTHER-IN-LAW: Hmmm. Okay, well, congratulations anyway!

Can you live with the reactions you might get from your mother-in-law, your best friend, and others when you tailor your announcement to your new philosophy of treating your twins as two separate babies? In announcing their upcoming birth in this nontraditional manner, you're telling everyone important to you how you want them to perceive the babies you are expecting. At the same time, you are reinforcing your own thinking about these babies and thus won't be as likely to fall into the habit of considering them solely as twins, halves of a whole. You are emphasizing the fact that they are going to be two separate and distinct babies, who will develop into two separate and distinct children, two separate and distinct teenagers, and two separate and distinct adults: siblings born on the same day but uniquely themselves.

Referring to each child as an individual will also help you to bond with each one because, by mentally focusing on each baby individually, your connection to each becomes stronger. With your initial recognition that each baby-to-be deserves to be thought of as an individual, you are making a promise to continue to perceive your baby in this way, which will strengthen his ability to develop a unique self.

When you announce that you're having two babies who will be born at the same time and you see that puzzled look on the faces of family members and friends, remind yourself of the priceless gift you are giving your babies. You are granting each of them the start in life that he or she deserves and that singleton children receive automatically: the birthright opportunity to be perceived as a single, special person.

Onesies, Cribs, and Showers

Mentally preparing to treat your two babies as individuals also entails some practical considerations. The physical accoutrements of babydom can have a significant influence on how you begin to think about your two babies and how each one comes to think of himself. Let's start with the babies' room.

Ideally, each baby would have his or her own room, but since most of us don't have the luxury of providing that, I recommend that, if space and finances permit, each baby have her own crib from the very beginning. The reason it's so important for each baby to have her own space is that it helps to create external boundaries; in other words, each child gets a sense of her separateness in an actual, physical way. Having separate cribs also encourages the family to acknowledge the distinctness of each baby. I suggest, as well, different color bedding and dissimilar crib toys. The two distinct sleeping quarters will help delineate your babies as two separate beings.

While many parents of twins and even some psychologists assert that infant twins need to sleep in the same crib at least for the first few months because they are accustomed to the presence of the other in utero, several studies related to infant attachment behavior demonstrate that babies need their parents, not their twin. They need to bond with the person responsible for nurturing them and attending to their needs, and that person is not their twin sibling but their parent.

We didn't have two separate rooms for Jonny and David because we had only planned for a fourth child. We did, however, borrow a crib and reused another one that our three older children had slept in, cramming both cribs into a tiny bedroom. It worked out fine. Some parents find that they need to place the cribs far enough apart from each other so that the babies won't wake each other up. One family I know decided to let one baby sleep in the den for the first year. A mother in one of my twins groups didn't have a spare room, but she did have a closet big enough for a crib, so she let one baby sleep in the closet for the first few months. Feel free to be flexible and creative as you plan for your twins' sleeping arrangements. The key here is to begin to treat your babies as separate beings and to allow them their own separate spaces.

When it comes to baby equipment, I think it is advantageous to have two of everything—within reason. Of course, two infant car seats are needed. But if space permits, each baby should also have his own dresser or at least his own separate drawers in the dresser. This spatial differentiation helps all family members realize and remember that these two babies are distinct and separate.

And then there is the matter of baby clothes, which brings us to the issue of the baby—or rather, babies—shower. Is it rude to impose your parenting-of-twins philosophy on shower guests who want to welcome your new babies with cute, matching outfits? In a word, no. If friends and family are organizing a shower for you, it will be up to you to communicate your "separate-and-distinct" perspective, and you can do this in a friendly way. Either you or the person organizing the shower will need to tell your guests to avoid buying similar or identical items because you want the babies to have their own unique identities, and clothing, even baby clothes, is part of that identity-building process. But be prepared for some negative feedback. Many of your well-meaning friends and relatives will be enormously disappointed that they won't be able to celebrate your twins by giving you adorable matching onesies, booties, sleepers, and overalls. Some may think you're a bit nuts for making such a big deal about the twin thing, and they will protest that matching pink and blue fuzzy sweaters are utterly harmless.

Of course, you will acknowledge that they're right. Dressing the twins similarly from time to time is fun and no big deal. However, you will also need to explain to them that there is a larger issue that you're concerned about: namely, the babies' developmental health. In order to maintain your belief in each baby's right to his own uniqueness, you are making it your policy to address his individuality with a zeal that, in the eyes of others, may border on the absurd. But caring about your babies' psychological health is not absurd, and neither is politely asking that shower guests bring gifts that honor each baby's singular identity. Again, let's see how such a clash of twin philosophies might play out:

YOU: I'm so happy you'll be coming to the shower. I just have one request: that your baby gifts be unmatching.

SHOWER GUEST: What do you mean? You're having twins, right?

YOU: Right. It's just that we want to start them off from day one with separate identities.

SHOWER GUEST: Don't you think you're carrying this a little far? How will they even know they're wearing matching outfits?

YOU: Well, you're right, they won't know at first. But the
more they appear to be alike, the more other people will
treat them as "the twins," rather than as two separate
babies. And we want each baby to feel good about just
being herself.

SHOWER GUEST: Okay—you win. So much for the matching
pink and lavender baby kimonos!

If you're not the conversationally assertive type, you might
want to consider simply writing something short, sweet, and to
the point on the shower invitation. For example,

> *Mom and Dad request that shower gifts celebrate
> each baby's uniqueness. The babies plan to go through
> life unmatching.*

Again, if your friends or family call wanting further explanation, explain that you are celebrating uniqueness rather than
twinness and that they can help by providing your babies with
"uniquely hers" or "uniquely his" baby items. Their efforts in
helping you to champion separateness will give both babies a
wonderful start in life. Be prepared, though, for those friends
and relatives who will do it their way and give you matching
outfits, regardless of your stated preference for unmatchingness.
A woman in one of my parents-of-twins groups told us about her
father, the grandfather to her five-year-old twins.

> *Even though I let everyone in my family know before
> the babies were born that we intended to dress them*

differently throughout their childhood, my father has sent matching outfits for every single one of the boys' birthdays. I've learned not to make a big deal out of it. I just laugh it off and let the boys' individual fashion choices take over. Since my husband and I have always dressed them differently, now that they're old enough to choose for themselves what they want to wear, they never choose grandpa's outfits on the same day anyway.

If, after the shower, your own shopping trips, and scouting for hand-me-downs, you find that you still don't have what you need to provide separate, unique clothing and other items for your babies, the National Organization of Mothers of Twins Club (NOMOTC) can help. NOMOTC is a nationwide group that helps mothers of twins cope with the myriad issues that beset mothers with newborn twins. They offer both emotional support and practical information regarding the overwhelming task of caring for two babies at the same time. Additionally, their local chapters are a great resource for locating all types of secondhand items. The cost of providing two cribs, two infant seats, two infant swings, and lots of nonmatching, used clothing that will be outgrown before you know it need not be prohibitive.

Preparing for Alone Time

As the parent of twins, you'll need the freedom to spend time alone with each baby as early as possible, and planning for it can begin before your babies are born. I believe strongly that spending as much time as possible alone with each baby is one of the essential ways to address each child's distinct needs, initiate distinct relationships with each one, and encourage each child to begin to develop a distinct self.

Before the babies arrive, I urge you to begin thinking about how such arrangements might be made. If your partner has a fairly flexible schedule, the two of you could work out times when each of you can take one baby out in the stroller while the other stays home with the other child. Or you might ask a friend or relative to stay with one baby while you take the other child out in the stroller or for an errand. Alone time with each baby need only entail a half-hour stroll or a quick errand—or as much time as you have coverage for the baby left at home. Then, of course, you'll have a similar out-of-the-house experience with the other baby. If it's not possible to have alone time with each baby outside the house, you can still have the one-on-one experience by simply going into another room and being alone together. The point is to be able to devote your attention solely and completely to one baby at a time.

The success stories relating to such arrangements will astound you, and we'll hear about them in the next chapter. At this point, it's not too early to begin planning for how you and your partner can make the alone-time schedule work for both of you.

When Darren and Alicia sat down to talk about how they might draw up an alone-time-with-each-baby plan, at first Darren balked at the idea. This is how Alicia remembered their initial discussion:

I liked the "alone-time-with-each-baby" idea, not just for the babies' sake but for my sake, too. I'd get a break from having to divide my attention—and have the chance to enjoy the "baby-and-me" experience rather than the constant "babies-and-me." But all Darren could think about was how much time all of this "alone time with one and then the other" was going to take. He was worried enough that the twins would be dominating our lives. If we each had to spend alone time with each baby, he felt it would take away from the little time we'd have together.

So I made him a deal. If he would agree to a flexible schedule of an hour two or three times a week, a half hour alone with each baby, I would enlist my sister and brother-in-law to babysit at least once a month so Darren and I could go out for dinner. At this point, he seems up for it. . . . We'll see how it goes once the babies arrive.

Most importantly about Alicia and Darren's discussion, they each brought their feelings out into the open and seemed to be able to hear each other's perspective, which enabled them to resolve their initial differences. Alicia picked up on Darren's concern about losing time together as a couple, so she committed to finding a potentially workable solution. And Darren got that being alone with each baby was important for their psychological well-being, as well as Alicia's.

As you approach your spouse with the alone-time-with-each-baby proposition, be aware that spending time alone with each child is a novel approach to parenting twins. Encourage your partner to express how he (or she) feels about it and give him time to adjust to the idea. (Lending him this book to read might be a good idea, too!)

An important piece of equipment you'll need for your alone time with each baby is a single stroller. A single stroller for the parent of twins? Absolutely. While it will be necessary to have a double stroller when you take both babies out at the same time, having access to a used, secondhand, or borrowed single stroller is also essential. It will remind you that each of your twins is a single baby who desires and needs to be with you alone. Granted, you could use the double stroller for your alone time with one baby, but the single stroller will serve as a physical reminder to treat each baby as precious in his own right.

When your partner, relative, neighbor, or nanny is available to take care of one baby, putting the other child in the single stroller and going out alone, just the two of you, will be a wonderful experience for both you and your baby. Rather than getting lots of attention and being bombarded with "twins" questions, you'll have some peaceful alone time with your "singleton" child and feel what it's like to be alone with just one baby. You will be able to focus on one little person and relish the joy and delight of devoting yourself exclusively to a single baby.

His and Hers Baby Books and Home Videos

While it's understandable that we all get caught up in the adorableness of seeing two babies together, we have to keep reminding ourselves that, as these babies become older children, each needs to be able to think of herself as her own unique person. One way that this single sense of oneself is revealed is through family photos. I think it is very important that each child be able to see pictures of herself alone, as well as pictures of herself alone with her parents and with her other siblings: in other words, photos of herself without her twin.

Getting caught up in the twin dynamic by taking lots of photos of your two babies together sets the stage for affording twinship a celebrity status. Although newborn babies will not yet be aware of it, they will eventually get the message that their being twins is more important than simply being who they are as individuals. It's what people are thrilled by and want to pay attention to. Certainly, you'll want to capture many glorious moments when the twins are together on film, but I suggest that you balance these with enough photos of each baby by herself, with another sibling, or with a parent. Again, the point is to celebrate each baby's uniqueness rather than her twin status. Remember, too, that as babies develop, the role of parents is to help each child become increasingly independent—from their parents as well as from their twin. The single baby photos on the mantel and in each child's baby book send a powerful message to the child: I exist on my own. I am important as an individual.

I created individual photo albums for each one of my children and then made a separate album for my husband and me that includes photos of all our children at different ages. Jonny and David have their own photo books, just like everyone else. Of course, there are delightful pictures of the two of them together, but they are interspersed with single photos of each boy and photos of each one with his siblings or with us. When they were born, a friend gave us two nonmatching picture frames engraved with their names so that each child was celebrated separately. I still treasure those.

As you're planning for the special baby items you'll want to have, think about two separate baby books and picture frames. They make a big difference in how your children view themselves, physically and emotionally.

Having a baby—or babies—is, of course, a time when most of us can't keep our hands off the video camera. As you make plans to film your babies for posterity, think about the need to capture singular moments that are not overshadowed by the adorable double images. The importance of these images of each child's individual personal history cannot be underestimated. When the babies are older, they will be aware of how they were initially seen as individuals and how much they were encouraged to be themselves.

Devising a Help-with-the-Twins Plan

Although many articles and books on the parenting of twins emphasize getting help with child care, many parents don't take the advice seriously. Or they arrange to get help only for the first month. You will need help for longer than that. So, it's not too early to think about whom you can call on for the first few months and beyond and how many hours a week you might be able to arrange with them. Then, come up with a help-with-the-twins tentative plan. Unless you have a plan, it will be that much more difficult to have time with each twin individually, time to yourself, time with your partner, or simply time to wash your hair. And if you have other children, the need to plan for outside help is even more crucial.

Your two babies will need to be fed, bathed, changed, dressed, put down for their naps, fed again, burped, held, sung to, rocked to sleep, and put down for the night—or part of the night anyway. Of course, all of this has its fun moments, but not if you don't get a chance to take a break. Just because you are lucky enough to have twins doesn't mean you aren't entitled to have some time alone to yourself, with neither baby in tow. But you'll need someone—or several someones—to help you out.

Help doesn't have to mean a full-time nanny. It can mean a babysitter two or three times a week for an hour or two, or a mother-in-law, sister, nephew, or neighbor who is trustworthy enough to take care of one or both twin infants for a short time. Any amount of help is beneficial, and if you don't have friends, neighbors, or family members you can call on, there are a number of other places from which to enlist support: community organizations, your church, synagogue, or mosque, even your twins support group. The sooner you organize your "support staff," the more relaxed you'll feel as you head toward delivery day.

Again, many mothers-to-be think they need to arrange for entire days of child-care help, but getting away by yourself even in small increments can do wonders to defrazzle you. And having even an hour of help a few times a week can also ensure that you'll be able to schedule some alone time with each twin.

If you have other children, and since twins are so often born prematurely, you'll also need to factor in the possible need for help with your older kids if you're involved with the babies in the neonatal intensive care unit. This may be for a week, a month, even three months, depending on how small the babies are when they're born or how critical their physical condition. So, you'll need to plan for someone or several people who can be there for your other children during this time, as well as when you bring the twins home from the hospital and are preoccupied with them. It's best if this helper is already close to your children (a grandparent, aunt or uncle, close friend, or trusted babysitter) so that things will transition as smoothly as possible. You may also need someone to oversee your other children if you are on bed rest during your pregnancy.

You'll look forward to the arrival of your babies with much more calmness and confidence when you devise a help-with-the-twins plan that assures you help is on the way.

Preparing the Siblings

One of our favorite, and most psychologically telling, family stories is that of our four-year-old daughter Amy's reaction to the news that she was going to have two younger brothers. "Name them Pee Pee and Poo Poo," she responded. It wasn't hard to decode Amy's x-rated response; she was angry. She liked being the baby, the youngest of three, and she didn't want to give up that prized position in our family. She was already competitive with her older sister, Sarah, who was six, and now she was thinking that she'd have to compete for attention with these babies. So, she had every reason to be upset.

It's important for you to understand how your older children feel about becoming a sister or brother to two new babies. First of all, you can sit down with them and ask how they feel about the news. After listening carefully to what they say, even if it's couched in an Amy-like pronouncement, you can begin both to reassure them and level with them about how their lives are going to change when the twins arrive. You might say something like this, tailoring your comments to the age of your child:

> *I know you're going to be a great help to me when the babies come home from the hospital, but I also know that getting used to them may be hard for you. Two new babies will make a big change in our family. They'll get a lot of attention, and there will be times when you won't like that, so you might feel mad at the babies or at me. But I'm really going to try to help you with your upset feelings as much as I can. And I'll still have time just for you. It's going to be hard for the first few months, but after a while we'll all get the hang of it. And the babies will be so happy to have a big brother/sister like you!*

A new baby in the family always steals the spotlight from the other child or children. With two babies, that spotlight is even brighter due to the special excitement everyone feels about twins. So, be sensitive to your older child's initial reactions and be prepared for her to feel angry, jealous, and anxious once the babies become part of your household. If you reassure her ahead of time that you understand how she feels, that you will help her deal with her feelings, and that she'll be a much-needed helper for her baby sisters/brothers, her adjustment to the babies, although still challenging, may be easier.

Amy loved being a big sister to her baby brothers, and her involvement in my pregnancy definitely had its perks. She and I have fond memories of watching the *Cinderella* video together (over and over again) when I was on modified bed rest for the last few weeks before the twins arrived. And we both know "A Dream Is a Wish Your Heart Makes" by heart.

Are You and Your Partner on the Same Parenting Page?

Like every other parenting decision you'll make in the next eighteen plus years, the one to consciously treat your twins as two separate individuals will be most effective if you and your spouse agree that it's the right way to go. But what if your partner doesn't take the parenting-of-twins philosophy outlined in this book as seriously as you do, or believes it only applies once the kids get older? "What difference could it possibly make," he or she might prod, "to let my parents buy the babies matching outfits as a shower gift?" In fact, a few matching outfits will make little difference in the overall emotional development of your babies; but the unmatching concept makes a big difference, and it's important that you and your partner generally see eye to eye on it. The key is for both of you to acknowledge that the individuality of each baby is something to be celebrated and nurtured.

As the two of you plan for the arrival of your babies, talk about why you believe that parenting your twins as individuals is so important. And discuss, too, how you would like to share child-care responsibilities in the first stages of your children's lives. Having twins provides an expanded opportunity for men to be involved with baby care since moms obviously need more help. And the importance of alone time with each baby is an added reason for dads to share primary caretaking with their wives. As for signing on to the strategies espoused in this book, in my experience with parents of twins, I've found that men are usually pleased to follow the wife's lead in the first year of the babies' lives. For example, if the wife lets her husband know that she's in favor of alone time with each baby, a strategy that some may characterize as radical and counterintuitive, he will likely be comfortable with it, too. If wives say, "I think it would benefit both babies if you took one out alone several times a week while I spent time alone with the other, and then we can switch off," husbands who want to be involved dads will usually be happy to go along with the program.

Fathers like having alone time with one baby, and they appreciate it when their wives delegate baby-care responsibilities. Rather than constantly having to ask what they can do to help or attempting to read their wives' minds, they prefer to know in advance what is expected of them and why it's important. Fathers of newborns are generally pleased to have an assignment and to feel useful and effective.

On the other hand, although fathers appreciate their new role as involved parent and caretaker of two new babies, it may be tough for some men to take orders from their wives. With two babies, moms seem to be endlessly giving orders and may not be very gentle or diplomatic when they do so. Or they may accuse their husbands of not doing "it"—changing, rocking, feeding, burping—the "right way," so fathers become angry or resentful or feel unappreciated. And, of course, most expectant fathers of twins worry that they'll be pushed aside by the babies, last in line for their wives' attention. So, like Alicia and Darren, it will be crucial for the two of you to talk about how you plan to set aside alone time for each other, even if it's just that monthly dinner out together.

Making plans now for time alone together, time alone with each baby, and time alone to yourself can go a long way toward preventing, or at least lessening, some of the inevitable marital clashes that arise as couples adjust to sharing their lives with two new babies. Discussing your parenting philosophy and proposed baby-care plans with your partner before the babies' arrival will help both of you feel more in the loop, less apprehensive, and closer to each other.

What's in a Name?

If you're a twin, plenty. Your name is your very own personal label, and unless you're a Charles the Third or a James Junior, it signifies your individuality. You might assume that since books on raising twins have been suggesting for over fifty years that twins not be given names that rhyme or start with the same letter, by now parents would have taken the advice to heart. Yet, in 2007 the Social Security Administration's list of the most popular twin names revealed that most twin pairs have matching names, like Taylor/Tyler, Hailey/Hannah, Matthew/Michael, Gabriella/Isabella, and Ethan/Evan. The most popular twin names for 2006 were Emma and Ella for girls and Jacob and Joshua for boys.[3]

3. United States Social Security Online, *Popular Names of Twins*, available at www.ssa.gov/OACT/babynames/twins.html (accessed May 15, 2007).

Perhaps you're thinking, what harm is there in giving twins alliterative names? They sound awfully cute, don't they? But is the sound of cute, matching names worth the potentially negative effect on two children who will answer to them for the rest of their lives? Tricia, thirty-seven, talked to me about what it was like going through life as a twin with a matching name.

> *My sister, Tina, and I are identical twins with very different lifestyles, although we share some of the same interests and are good friends. There were a lot of things growing up, though, that grated on me— the jokes about not being able to tell us apart, the branding (I was "the artistic twin" and Tina was "the athletic twin"). But the name thing really got on my nerves. Not only do our names almost sound alike, but somehow we got this nickname in kindergarten, and it stuck: "the two Ts," or "Tooties." I was so embarrassed by it. Not to mention that I essentially lost my name; I was just part of this jokey twosome. I never had the nerve to say anything about it. Besides, how does a five-year-old stand up to something like that?*

When Jane and I were growing up, there were a lot of family members who couldn't tell us apart, so someone came up with the conjoined name "Ja-on" (pronounced "Jay-own"). I guess this made it easier for them and prevented the self-consciousness that came with not being able to tell who was who. But the name that wasn't my name made me feel that no one knew who I really was. There was no "me"; I was just part of a unit. Since Jane and I looked so much alike, I at least wanted my own name, even if no one got it right. I longed for a name that was different enough from my sister's so that people would know me for who I was.

When twins are given names that sound like a pair, it reinforces a potent, yet unspoken, message: the two of you are connected forever; your twinness is your identity. "Jacob and Joshua" may sound harmonious, but to twins the sound becomes emotionally clanging. Parents' attraction to the practice of giving twins matching names is another example of how tantalizing the twin mystique can be, even to those who pay lip service to supporting each twin's separateness and uniqueness. As you and your partner pour over the baby-naming books and discuss potential names for your two new children, keep in mind that you will be granting each of them a lasting favor by selecting names that they can embrace as uniquely theirs.

Parents-of-Twins Journal:
Mentally Preparing for Two Separate Babies

In every chapter from here on, you'll have the chance to interact with the material just presented. Use a small journal or spiral notebook to enter your responses.

WRITE DOWN YOUR THOUGHTS

- What are the greatest barriers to thinking of your twins-to-be as two separate babies? What aspects of the twin mystique do you still find appealing or difficult to relinquish?

- What benefits do you think your babies will derive from your treatment of them as separate children? How does the thought of providing those benefits make you feel?
- What worries you most about parenting two babies at the same time?
- What are you most looking forward to about having two babies at the same time?

Tips for Expectant Parents of Twins

- Sit down with your spouse and devise a workable plan for each of you to spend alone time with each baby. The more prepared you are ahead of time, the less frazzled you'll be when your babies arrive—and the more benefit your children will derive from the alone time spent with each of you.
- Make sure to arrange for enough outside help for the first few months of your babies' lives. If a nanny or babysitter is beyond your budget, compile a list of trusted friends, relatives, or neighbors who might be willing to pitch in, even for an hour or two a week.
- In compiling necessary baby items, don't forget to include a single stroller so that you can take each baby out separately during your alone times with each one.
- As you get ready to bring two new babies into your family, continue to think about each child as a distinct individual whom you will get to know and cherish as his or her own unique person.

• three •

BABYHOOD

My best friend tries to be helpful by giving me advice based on what worked with her daughters. But people who've had one baby at a time don't understand the emotional demands of having twins. I feel guilty for spending too much time with one and not the other. I feel that Carrie, who is so sweet and tranquil, is being penalized because I have to give so much attention to Willie, who cries a lot and is much more demanding. Then I feel like an evil mom for holding it against Willie. I'm totally dependent on our babysitter, yet plagued by the idea that Carrie may be growing closer to her than to me. And I rarely get to enjoy any quiet moments of bonding with either baby because I'm always thinking about the one I'm not with!

—BETH, MOTHER OF NEWBORN TWINS

Welcome to the real world of parenting twins. In addition to the expected joy and exhaustion, having two babies unexpectedly ushers in feelings of guilt, inadequacy, concerns about fairness, and overall emotional overload.

Not only are you dealing with the nonstop physical needs of two new babies and being called upon to intuit and decipher two different infant temperaments, but the sheer enormity of the job makes you doubt your competence and effectiveness as a mother or father. And if such pressures aren't enough, preterm births and complicated deliveries, common with twins, mean that your babies may have required hospitalization in the neonatal intensive care unit. So, prior to coming home from the hospital, you may have already faced obstacles that most parents of singletons don't have to contend with. The bottom line is, you are more than entitled to feel exceptionally overwrought and overwhelmed.

Still, most parents of twins are ashamed to admit feeling inundated by their role as caretaker of two babies. This is especially true for those who went through infertility treatments and believe that anything other than intense bliss and gratitude is an unacceptable emotion. Then there are the mothers like me, who gave birth to singletons before having twins and are shocked to discover that being mom to two babies is a vastly different experience than mothering one. My first night home with the boys made it frightfully clear that I would not be able to manage two babies on my own for at least six months. So much for supermom.

In this chapter, we'll explore ways to deal with the perfectly normal, yet incredibly disorienting, "overwhelmed-by-two-babies" phase of twin parenting. The philosophy and strategies explored in the previous two chapters are key not only to doing what's best for you and your babies but to enjoying their fascinating, yet fleeting, babyhood.

First, let's take a closer look at the emotional state in which most parents of twins find themselves when two new babies join the family.

Emotional Overload

When Kim attended her first session of our mothers-of-twins group, her story highlighted some common emotional conflicts that arise in a new parent of two babies. After getting into a minor car accident due to shattered nerves and fatigue and being told by her physician that she should begin taking antidepressants, Kim became convinced that she needed emotional support. A successful advertising executive in her mid-thirties, she had become pregnant with the help of fertility drugs after she and her husband tried to conceive on their own for several years. She chose to retire from her profession to be a full-time stay-at-home mom. But after only a few months at home with her fraternal twin sons, Kim wasn't sure how she would get through the next few days, let alone the coming years.

> *I have been absolutely stunned by my inability to adjust to my new role as the mother of twins. I'm a resilient, competent person, or at least I thought I was, and I usually learn quickly and adapt well to new situations. So why am I having such a hard time with these two adorable little creatures? I'm a wreck—and I feel horribly guilty about it. I have full-time help, a supportive husband, and the luxury of not having to return to work. What's my problem? And what's the secret—because I obviously haven't found it!*

While I assured Kim there was no hidden secret to adjusting to the emotional upheaval of parenting twins, I promised she would learn about a parenting philosophy that would help. But first, each of us in the group shared our personal "combat stories" about our less-than-perfect adjustment to our new babies. These frank accounts of dealing with two infants at once would allow Kim to realize she was not alone.

I told Kim that my overriding emotion during the first twenty-four hours of taking care of my baby boys was shock. I had expected few difficulties when I brought them home from the hospital, having been through the infant stage three times before. But after one night of attempting to care for both babies, I was on the verge of mental and physical collapse. My husband and I decided to hire nighttime help to allow us time to recuperate. And even after having help at night for the first six months, I was still uneasy about my ability to perform my maternal duties.

Sandra told Kim how disappointed she had felt; caring for her twins was definitely not the warm, nurturing experience she'd had with her singleton daughter. Nursing her older daughter had involved wonderful shared moments of intimacy and contentment, but there seemed to be no way she could have those experiences with her twin daughters. Denise explained that caring for both her daughters seemed burdensome and oppressive; she had never felt that way when caring for her two older singleton sons. Brenda added that she felt guilty that she was not enjoying the experience of parenting her twins and worried that this meant she did not love her children. Janice revealed that she felt fortunate to be able to go to work because she was so overwhelmed and out of control that leaving the house and focusing on her job was the only way she could regain a sense of herself as a competent person. Cindy succinctly expressed how frustrated she felt after her twins were born, saying, "It was the feeling of never catching up, never doing enough, never having enough sleep, never finding sufficient time for either child, and never feeling competent or fulfilled."

Kim was relieved to know that her emotional reactions to parenting twin babies weren't that far off from ours, and she was happy to have a place where she could "vent" about all the upsetting changes she was going through. However, if our sharing of troubling emotions surrounding the initial twin-parenting experience sounds like a pity party, let me explain. It is my firm belief that new parents of twins must be able to express honestly what they're going through—and a forum such as a parents-of-twins group is the perfect place. But thanks to the twin mystique, as well as the notion that previous infertility patients should feel nothing other than grateful, parents of twins often keep their negative emotions to themselves. Or they take their frustrations out on their spouses, their other children, or themselves. So, opening up about what you're experiencing and feeling is a crucial first step toward raising emotionally healthy twins. Ambivalent feelings about parenting your babies are normal and have nothing to do with not loving or caring about your children.

Getting back to Kim's initial plea, what about the "secret" that might make the experience of parenting twins more manageable and more fulfilling—and more beneficial to your twins?

Bonding with Each Baby during Alone Time

I discovered the "secret" of alone time with each baby out of necessity, and if necessity is the mother of invention, I was one mother in desperate need. My story is somewhat typical. I arrived home with my baby boys and hoped to settle into some sort of routine. Having already parented three infants, I knew enough to expect that day and night would be indistinguishable for a while. I was not prepared, however, for the anxiety and despair that I felt about the "inequality" of my feelings toward Jonny and David. Jonny was a calm, easygoing baby. Our older kids still laugh when they recall him nestled contentedly in his infant seat while David wailed unceasingly in the next room. David had colic and was miserable.

I planned to use formula along with intermittent breast-feeding and was able to breast-feed Jonny without difficulty, but I could not nurse David. After my many unsuccessful attempts, I switched him to formula full-time. Sadly, I felt as if I had a tenuous connection with David. He was usually fed by the babysitter or my husband, and when he wasn't eating, he was most often uncomfortable and crying because he was in distress.

It was strange and upsetting to feel so out of sync with my babies. I believed in my capacity to attune to each child, but now I was only able to meet some of each twin's needs, and this seemed to happen only in sporadic moments as I waited to care for the other one. I felt there simply wasn't enough of me to satisfy two babies. My ability to experience, intuit, and know each of my babies was severely handicapped by the presence of the other child. I longed for the serene, fulfilling moments, the "I-feel-empowered-and-in-control-as-a-mother" moments.

I would ask myself, what is Jonny about? who is David? but I had limited mental space in which to find the answers because the constant presence of two babies made such discoveries feel impossible. Without exclusive time with each baby, I couldn't begin to unravel my unique connection to each. When the boys were about six weeks old, I decided I had to create a special space away from the other baby so that I could be with one child at a time and really get to know each of them separately.

So, how did I begin my experiment in alone time with each baby? I took Jonny for a walk in the single stroller. It felt so nice to be just the two of us. We'd walk down our street, and I'd talk to him and thank him for being so patient. And I'd just appreciate being with him. Our alone time gave us a connection we couldn't have at home because I was so distracted by the other children's needs, and especially by David. My initial alone times with David usually consisted of putting him in his car seat, even if he was screaming, and being alone with him while I drove to pick up my older children at elementary school. I'd turn on the car radio to some soothing music, or I'd talk to him as we were driving, and this gave us an experience that wasn't all about my trying to satisfy his needs. It was just a time to be together. Sometimes I took Jonny with me to go grocery shopping and was thrilled not to receive the special twins attention; it was just me smiling and talking to Jonny about which apples to buy and him smiling back. I took David in a Snugli for walks in our neighborhood, with me feeling more confident about being able to soothe him and him relaxing a bit, snug against mom's chest. Almost every day, I took alone time with one or the other baby, whoever was awake when I had twenty minutes for a walk or when I had an errand to do.

I had found a solution to the profound problem of not feeling sufficiently connected to either baby. I needed these opportunities to be alone with each child as much as each of them needed to be alone with me. Our alone-time outings helped mitigate my hopelessness about not being able to quell David's colic, my despair about showering much more attention on David and ignoring Jonny, and my confusion about feeling split in my role as a mother and caretaker.

My success with the alone-time strategy motivated me to encourage my clients to try it as well. This simple plan has proven to be the most effective antidote to parental feelings of frustration, inadequacy, and ineffectualness brought on by the experience of parenting twins. The parents in my private practice and in my parents-of-twins groups came to appreciate that this precious time alone with each baby helped to create a necessary bond between parent and child and enabled parents to feel that they were providing each child with what they needed most—exclusive attention from mom or dad.

Each parent discovers his or her own way of making the alone-time strategy work. One mom in our group brings one of her twins with her to the supermarket because he enjoys sitting in the shopping cart and pointing to all the items on the shelves. She doesn't bring his brother shopping because he is too active and doesn't like to sit still for very long, but she finds that a separate outing with him to a nearby bookstore is more suited to his temperament. There's a special place in the bookstore with a big rug, lots of soft cloth baby books, and plenty of space for babies to crawl around. One dad likes to take walks with his baby to a nearby construction site where the baby absolutely loves watching the dump trucks scooping up dirt. When the dad is alone with the other baby, they enjoy going to the park and watching the older kids play basketball. And Beth, who initially complained that she had only fleeting moments to bond with one or the other baby, found that once she scheduled regular alone times with each child, doing such simple activities as taking a short walk or driving to the drugstore, she could finally enjoy being alone with one baby without worrying about depriving the other of her attention.

The best way to begin to establish a secure attachment with each baby is to find out what your baby is like away from, and not in comparison with, her sibling. Each baby is a unique person and needs you to focus on her alone whenever you can create the opportunity to do so. Unless one of your babies doesn't like being in a stroller, the single stroller can be your ticket to alone time. When you take out one baby at a time for a stroll, you won't be bombarded by well-intentioned onlookers fascinated with your twins. Instead, each child will have those precious moments of time alone with you when, thanks to your exclusive attention to her, she can get to know you—and herself.

Of course, in order to enjoy alone time with each baby, you'll need to have someone—your spouse or a relative, friend, or paid professional—to care for your other child. Ideally, it's best if you can set up a regular schedule with your helper so that you know you'll have alone time with each baby on certain days at certain times. Getting out of the house and being alone with each baby as often and as consistently as you can will go a long way toward building a meaningful connection with each child and defusing your initial "parent-of-twins emotional overload."

Resistance to Alone Time

Even when parents of twins believe wholeheartedly in the importance of nurturing their children's individual identities, and even though they may long for exclusive time with their babies beyond basic caretaking duties, there is a certain resistance to undertaking the alone-time strategy for several reasons. First of all, the need for parents to prove their parental competence may inhibit them from spending time alone with each child. There is the sense that they desperately wanted these babies and they are determined to show that they can handle caring for both of them at the same time. Another factor is a parent's concern about attaching herself or himself equally to each baby. Although parents may acknowledge that it's natural to have different responses to their babies' distinct temperaments and demands, they still worry that if they spend time alone with each child, they might bond with one more than the other and thus be guilty of "unequal" treatment. A third reason is that the twin mystique feeds the erroneous notion that separating twins is somehow unhealthy. Parents are led to believe that if they separate their babies even for relatively short periods of time, the sibling bond will be diminished or harmed.

When I first brought up the "alone-time-with-each-baby" strategy in my parenting groups, I was met with such reactions as, "It's not right to split them up!" "How do I decide who goes and who stays?" "What if the other baby is angry?" I had to assure these well-meaning parents that it's extremely important for every baby to get that exclusive attention from his mother and from his father so that the baby can form a one-to-one relationship with each parent. If the twins are always together, thus always dividing the attention of the parent, the connection to each twin's parent that every baby needs might become problematic.

Alone time will actually make you feel less guilty about constantly having to divide yourself in half and relieve you of the sense that you're not meeting either child's needs or that you're meeting one baby's needs more than the other's. When you spend one-on-one time separately with each of them, you fill yourself up with good feelings rather than with guilty or conflicted ones. The payoff for taking care of a baby's physical needs is the emotional satisfaction and fulfillment you get from bonding with him. Alone time with each child facilitates closeness.

Sometimes it takes an unavoidable circumstance to legitimize alone time. Lynette talked about how wonderful it was to have a "legitimate" reason to spend time alone with her eighteen-month-old daughter, Chloe.

> *When Chloe needed minor surgery, I stayed with her in the hospital for three days and was so surprised by what a wonderful experience it was. I finally had the chance to get to know her on her own terms, apart from her twin brother. It was one of the first times the two of us actually got to be with each other without any interruptions (other than the hospital staff). We talked and played games, I read her her favorite stories, and we enjoyed the hospital meals together. In those three days we really got close. I finally gave myself permission to be alone with my daughter.*

It's a shame that Lynette had to wait eighteen months to justify being alone with each of her twins, but the hospital experience convinced her of the benefits of alone time. As for the worry about bonding more with one than the other, this comes back to two important concepts in our new philosophy of parenting twins: expect to have different feelings for each child, and don't attempt to provide a "fair-and-equal" childhood for your twins. Parents struggle needlessly in order to be fair to each baby, and they suffer with guilt when one baby needs more time than the other, believing that equal time is a must. What babies actually need at this point in their lives is neither equality nor togetherness with their twin; they need a secure attachment with each parent. Spending alone time with each baby helps parents celebrate each child rather than feeling guilty about inequality or unfairness.

I remember being alone with Jonny and feeling loving toward him for being such a terrific baby. Spending time together away from David helped me recognize my gratitude for Jonny's patience and serenity. Being alone with David after his colic abated was a joy. He was an exuberant baby who enjoyed our alone times. I really got to know what David was about in our outings together because I attuned exclusively to him and his needs.

It is more of a challenge to bond with two babies at the same time, and one cannot love two babies in exactly the same way because each baby is different. To imagine that we can do so is to erase their unique personalities as well as our own. Being honest with ourselves about what we enjoy and appreciate in each of our babies enables us to give them the exclusive attunement they deserve.

If you feel guilty about growing closer to one baby, if you worry about treating them equally or are concerned that others may think it's wrong to split them up, remember that these are your issues, not your babies'. What they need most is time with you—alone. So don't let your qualms hold you back from giving your babies what they require to develop a healthy emotional foundation.

Preferring One
Baby over the Other

One of the core emotional dilemmas facing most new parents of twins is how to deal with the guilt over feeling more attached to one baby than the other. It is natural to expect that a sleep-deprived mother of twins will appreciate the baby who needs her less. The more demanding infant will require more of her, while the more contented one is appreciated for being more easily regulated. On the other hand, it's possible that the baby who needs mother less will become less attached to her if mother comes to think of his independence as rejecting or unloving. Or mother may reward the more easily contented baby with special feelings. Or, as the babies mature and become more easily regulated, the dynamic may play out differently.

The point is that parents of newborn twins need to understand the challenges of bonding with two babies and that their relationship to each child is fluid and changeable. The healthiest way to negotiate this initial phase of getting to know each of your babies is to be honest and authentic in acknowledging your feelings. One mom in our mothers-of-twins group shared that she felt terrible complaining about one baby's irritability while guiltily looking forward to holding and cuddling the other baby. Yet, if we cannot complain, that is, be open about our less-than-warm-and-fuzzy feelings, we are susceptible to distorting the truth of our experience and displacing our uneasy feelings elsewhere.

When parents acknowledge that they prefer one baby over the other for various reasons, they not only unburden themselves of troubling feelings, but they can take whatever steps might be necessary to avert a potential problem. When you're open with yourself about why you might prefer one baby over the other, you can put those preferences in perspective and more readily accept that your feelings will fluctuate throughout your children's childhood.

Some parents are so upset by their feelings of favoring one baby over the other that they can't even acknowledge or discuss the emotional turmoil they're going through. Many insist that they have no preference, that they love both babies the same. But preferring the company of one baby over the other doesn't really have anything to do with love. Showing a preference for one baby at certain times is a way to cope with the overwhelming caretaking tasks required of a parent with two new babies. Also, preferences reveal the distinctions between two babies whose relationships to you and whose emerging personalities are unique and in flux. Jonny was happy gazing into space, while David screeched and wailed, but these descriptions in no way typify their personalities today or reveal how much my husband and I loved them then—or now.

Is it wrong to prefer the baby who is less demanding? Is it unforgivable to be frustrated with the baby who feeds so slowly? Is it sinful to feel victimized by a baby's colic screaming? Is it unhealthy to be grateful that one baby is more easygoing? Having a preference for one baby or the other in these early months of their lives is not a bad thing at all; in fact, it can be a good thing because it helps parents feel a differentiated connection to each baby. And feeling connected to each one is what's most important. Too often parents unwittingly abdicate their connection to each baby in favor of connecting to the two as a set because they feel guilty about having unequal feelings toward them. When parents are uncomfortable having different feelings for

each baby, they may lump the two together, physically and emotionally, which jeopardizes each child's need for a separate relationship with his or her parent.

Preferring to be with one or the other baby at particular
times is not necessarily negative. Deciding which twin to take to
the market, to bring to the park, to go for a walk with, or to read
a book to does not imply more or less love for one or the other
child. It is simply a way to choose how to be alone with each baby.

The Urge to Compare

As I mentioned earlier, labeling one twin's behavior according to
how it compares to the other's begins as an innocent means of
differentiating between the two. This can happen as early as
when the twins are fetuses being viewed on the ultrasound ("the
pushy one" versus "the placid one") or when they're newborns
("the easygoing one" versus "the demanding one"). In our family David was the twin who "cried all the time" and Jonny was
"contented and easygoing." David was "the needy baby," and
Jonny was "the good baby."

What feelings and experiences led me to come up with these
labels? I felt badly that David was so distressed, and I felt helpless
about having so much difficulty soothing him. I tried my best and
then handed him over to someone else to give him a bottle. I felt
badly that I spent less time with Jonny because it was so much
easier to feed him and put him to sleep. And because he didn't
fuss when he had to wait his turn, I attended to him last. If David
woke up at night, I was annoyed because it took so long to soothe
him back to sleep. If Jonny's crying woke up David, I was annoyed about anticipating a trying night. I prayed Jonny wouldn't
need anything because I was so exhausted being up with David.

My feelings of resentment toward David and my hoping that he wouldn't need me created an emotional dilemma. His neediness caused me to miss out on spending equal time with Jonny, who was thus shortchanged. If I hadn't acknowledged my conflicting emotions, it would have been easy to simply allow the shorthand labels to define our sons' newborn personalities: Jonny, the "good" twin "victimized" by his "needy," "difficult" brother, David.

Such early perceptions might have distorted my capacity to relate to each twin as he really was because the labels reflected that I was only perceiving David and Jonny in a comparative way. Fortunately, those one-word descriptions didn't define my boys because my husband and I spent alone time with each baby and got to know them beyond such simplistic labels. When parents try to spend alone time with each twin and have the chance to get to know each baby as a single child, it is less likely that each will be defined by one-dimensional, comparative labels rather than by an array of more nuanced behaviors.

Brenda's story illustrates how twin comparisons can lead to parental resentment, which undermines the newly forming parent-child bond. Brenda's one-year-old twins, Evan and Rebecca, couldn't have been more different. Evan was more relaxed and fit well into the family style of going places and doing active things. Rebecca was described as being "born anxious." Even as a newborn, she would whimper and frown in her sleep. Brenda had become increasingly intolerant of Rebecca's anxiety because it interfered with the family's functioning as a unit. She told me that she felt like screaming for Rebecca to "get over it!" because she was so annoyed by constantly having to deal with her baby daughter's intense insecurity. Comparing Rebecca to Evan made Rebecca's behavior seem even worse. Evan rolled with the punches and easily adapted to new situations, whereas Rebecca desperately clung to Brenda whenever they were in a new environment, cried when her grandparents went to pick her up, and awakened from her naps screaming.

After our sessions, Brenda began to realize that it was her responsibility as a parent to attune to Rebecca as a one-year-old individual who was experiencing anxiety, rather than as someone who didn't behave like her brother and who didn't easily fit in with the family program. Brenda admitted that she constantly compared Rebecca to Evan, which made her even more frustrated with Rebecca. If Evan had no problem being picked up by grandpa or taken to a new place, Brenda had wondered, what was Rebecca's problem?

Brenda saw that she might have attuned to Rebecca's anxious personality with more empathy if Rebecca had been born a singleton. But the physical and emotional stress of caring for two babies, added to the constant comparisons between Rebecca's and Evan's behavior, made Brenda feel frustrated, angry, and resentful.

Of course, parents of singletons must also relate to their child on their own terms, without trying to force them to fit in with particular family expectations. The difference is that parents of twins have the added challenge of staying attuned to two separate babies while at the same time attending to their overwhelming needs and demands. Also, parents of singletons, even when sleep deprived and anxious, have more opportunity to take comfort in those awe-inspiring moments of joy and delight that caring for a baby includes, and it is these positive experiences that enable them to nurture their baby lovingly even in the worst of times. Parents of newborn twins have very few one-on-one parent and child moments. Without time alone with each baby, mothers and fathers have less opportunity to feel the joys of their singular connection, yet it is precisely this connectedness that allows them to know their babies—not so much by what they need as by who they are.

Brenda was encouraged by my recommendation that she spend more alone time with Rebecca. She recognized that comparing Rebecca to Evan was not only unfair but prevented her from learning more about Rebecca, attending to her needs, and strengthening her connection to her. Brenda came to understand that giving up the urge to compare and getting to know Rebecca through a one-to-one mother-baby relationship, even for a few hours a week, would help Brenda meet her daughter's needs and, just as importantly, enjoy her company.

If you find yourself comparing your twins, wishing one were more like the other, feeling frustrated that Baby A isn't developing as brilliantly as Baby B, then you are not alone. On the path toward giving up "comparison parenting," the parents in my groups have shared their stories of the needless frustration that comparing two babies includes. Here are just a few such scenarios:

- Diana felt pressured to take baby Jeremy to a physical therapist because he wasn't living up to his brother Jackson's accomplishments. Jackson had recently learned to pull himself up and take a few steps, but Jeremy hadn't yet begun to do so.
- Candace worried that her ten-month-old daughter, Mara, was not developing along with her bruiser brother, Todd, who navigated so easily in his Grip 'n Go

baby walker. She was concerned that Mara was too stereotypically "girly" because she wasn't athletic like Todd and fell down all the time. Candace wanted her to stay competitive with her brother.

- Hilary was concerned about why it was taking fourteen-month-old Kaitlin so long to give up her bottle when her twin sister, Ellie, had gone on to more "mature" behavior months before.

Each of these parents learned to throw away the measuring stick that computes a baby's development and personality solely by comparing him to his twin, and I encourage you to toss out the comparison yardstick as well. Avoid the temptation to compare such babyhood milestones as, who was born first? who weighed more? who lifted up his head first? who smiled first? who walked first? or who got the first tooth? The opportunities for comparisons are endless, so make the commitment now to reject this particular twin-parenting trap. You'll be honoring each child and promoting his emotional well-being when you refuse to give in to the urge to compare and, instead, discover and respect each baby's unique self.

Is My Baby Closer to Our Housekeeper Than to Me?

Danielle joined our group when her fraternal twin daughters were a few months old. These were her first children, conceived naturally and born without complications. Happily married and in her mid-thirties, Danielle had been self-employed but made the decision to quit working after the twins were born because she wanted to be very involved in their lives. Since she was the product of a divorced home, without close ties to her parents, siblings, or relatives, she especially looked forward to creating a close, loving family.

Danielle hadn't planned to have help with the babies, but after a few days, she realized that there was no way she could handle the baby-care responsibilities by herself. Her husband was available and supportive when he returned home from work late in the evening, but she needed assistance during the day. Panic-stricken about all that was required of her in taking care of two babies, she hired a housekeeper for several hours every day and was relieved to have an extra pair of hands helping her feed the babies, do the laundry, change the babies, get them to sleep, and get some semblance of a meal on the table for her husband and herself.

One evening, Danielle appeared at our meeting teary eyed as she began to tell us about the relationship that was developing between her daughter, Lily, and Consuela, the housekeeper.

> Lily's eyes light up when Consuela arrives in the morning. I'll be feeding her and she'll pull away and start whimpering for Consuela. When Consuela takes Lily into her arms, I get a horrible pang of jealousy, even though I am now free to take care of Elise. I honestly feel that Lily is more attached to Consuela than she is to me and that somehow I have failed her as a mother.

While this particular concern is common among parents of singletons as well, it is even more troublesome to a parent of twins since bonding with two babies at once is more challenging. Not only is there the time constraint and emotional challenge of managing double caretaking duties, but there is also the worry over treating both babies equally.

So, even when there is someone like Consuela helping out, parents like Danielle feel upset about not being able to be the consistent, all-things-to-both-babies caretaker. On top of parental guilt about the babies' having to take turns for mom's or dad's attention, inevitable feelings of rivalry surface when a loving helper or nanny is on the scene. One mom told me that when she was in the babies' bedroom putting one twin down for a nap, she felt sad and upset to hear her other baby laughing with the nanny. "I had never heard her laugh like that," she said, "and I'm her mom!"

Many of the mothers of twins whom I have worked with are apologetic about or ashamed of needing a helper. A mother's feelings of inadequacy and shame over her inability to do it all on her own reflect the unrealistic expectations that our culture still places on women, liberated or not. But far from being shameful, arranging for adequate help is one of the healthiest gifts that new parents of twins can provide for their babies. Rather than being a sign of inadequacy, it is the gift of foresight and love. It is a promise to your babies, essentially telling them, "I will provide you with the necessary caretaking help so that I can be available to each of you in as many ways as I can."

I told Danielle that having twins is not about proving to the world that you can do it all. Providing your babies with an extra helper will give you more opportunity to interact individually with each baby. I encouraged Danielle to begin planning alone times with Elise and with Lily so that she could begin to build a closer relationship to each one, which would help to allay her jealous feelings toward Consuela.

If you find yourself grappling with a similar jealousy, remember that it is unnecessary for you and for your babies to turn the first year of their lives into a contest between you and your helper. Instead, consider the parenting helper as a participant in a collaborative effort that will ensure the well-being of your babies, as well as more time for you to be alone with each of them.

Why Your Babies Need Separate Experiences

According to the twin mystique, twins don't want to be, and shouldn't be, separated, and if parents go against this alleged wisdom, the twinship will somehow be damaged. In fact, just as siblings need breaks from one another, twins need separate experiences as well—perhaps even more so. If your babies are given the opportunity to experience themselves away from their twin sibling, they will have a better understanding that reality extends beyond "me and my twin." They will discover who they are apart from their same-age sibling. Babies don't really begin to interact with each other until they're about six to ten months old, which underscores the misconception that they miss each other at this age.

While it may be hard for you, as the parent of twin babies, to project twenty years down the line, the following story may serve as a cautionary tale.

A friend of mine is acquainted with identical twin men who live together and also work together as caterers. They swim at the local YMCA and always share the same lane. They joke with my friend that they enjoy the same movies and the same rock groups, share season tickets to basketball games, and prefer double-dating young women who are either sisters or best friends.

Their parents sent them to different colleges, but one ended up transferring in order to be with the other.

Some parents of twins might hear this story and think, this just proves that twins don't like to be separated! What's missing from the twin swimmers' story, however, is the reason why they're inseparable. One possible explanation is that, when twins fail to become attached to their mother or father as babies, their primary attachment is to each other. They parent each other because they have not had a "secure attachment" with their primary caregiver. Since the twin mystique persists in holding up twinship as a mysteriously wonderful and unparalleled spiritual bond, twins who have never been separated can continue their joined-at-the-hip relationship without much social stigma. Sadly, this coupled lifestyle means that each person misses out on the opportunity to choose a self-determined, independent life or even to know that such a possibility exists.

So, it's not too early to make sure that your babies are offered opportunities to enjoy separate experiences. My husband and I planned separate activities for Jonny and David from the time they were born. Since they were together most of the day, we sensed that they would benefit from a break from one another every few days. And being out alone with each of them gave my husband and me a stronger feeling of connectedness to each baby.

Our plan to take them to separate "mommy-and-me" and "daddy-and-me" activities and gymnastic classes worked beautifully. I looked forward to being with Jonny so that I could watch how he handled himself away from his brother. He tended to be a bit reserved and cautious at first, but after a while he became quite comfortable in the company of other babies. I marveled at his intensity and his particular attention to details.

None of the other parents knew that he had a twin brother at home, and no one needed to know. He was known simply for being Jonny, not David's twin.

It was delightful for me to be alone with David at the gym class. He was outgoing and gregarious, enjoying the stimulation, music, and activities. No one knew that David had a twin brother, and no one bothered us with questions about why he was so much smaller than his twin. Those alone moments with David and with Jonny were precious and defining. I could watch each of them intently, mirror them, delight in them. My husband and I each had the time and emotional space to focus completely on "baby and me." And each baby had the opportunity to experience life as a little individual out in the world making his own amazing discoveries.

Breast-feeding—or Not

One of the most pressing issues for new mothers of twins is whether or not to breast-feed. Many moms consider breast-feeding to be the optimal way to feed their infants since health-care specialists agree that mother's milk is the most beneficial food for newborns. As for the experience of breast-feeding, it can be a wonderful way to bond with your baby; for some mothers, however, it can be difficult and even painful. As might be expected, breast-feeding two babies is a very different experience from breast-feeding one. If you breast-feed both babies at the same time, you might be highly revered by other moms.

If you breast-feed one baby at a time, you will get that alone time with each child, but you may not fully enjoy it if you are constantly thinking about the one who is waiting to be nursed (or bottle-fed if he or she is having a problem nursing, as my baby David had). Parents of twins experience the inevitable fatigue of feeding two babies whichever method they choose, but unless you have sufficient help or a workable feeding plan—and an "I-promise-to-be-easy-on-myself" attitude—guilt and frustration can arise due to worries about one baby's waiting his turn while the other one is fed.

Regardless of how many babies are involved, breast-feeding isn't always as easy or as automatic as we are led to believe. Contrary to romanticized expectations, it can take time to acclimate to a breast-feeding routine. When it works, it brings rewarding benefits for both mom and baby, but sometimes it doesn't work out despite a mother's best intentions. The most important thing for new moms to remember is not to allow your self-esteem to rest on your ability to breast-feed. Mothers of twins don't need any more pressure than they already have, and pressuring yourself to take on the breast-feeding of two babies when it is unfeasible for whatever reason is not emotionally healthy for you or your twins. If you cannot breast-feed your twins and feel like a failure because of it, your infants will suffer not from the lack of your breast but from your downcast mood. More important than whether they get nourishment from a breast or a bottle is the quality of attention they receive from you in the form of emotional sustenance. Your babies will be fine whether you feed them breast milk, formula, or a combination of the two. Bonding with a baby is not all about the breast.

I know from my own experience that close maternal bonds can be created regardless of how you feed your twins. Having breast-fed my three older children, I didn't feel compelled to repeat the experience with Jonny and David. Also, given the demands of my other children, exclusive breast-feeding of the twins wasn't a viable option. As it turned out, David's colic made breast-feeding impossible, so he was strictly bottle-fed, and Jonny had modified breast-feeding. Both experiences were satisfying but different. The most gratifying aspect was my ability to spend time with each baby.

Unfortunately, too many women feel a sense of inadequacy about not breast-feeding, as if it were the ultimate badge of femininity and maternal success. But if breast-feeding presents logistical or physical problems, or if you simply are unable to breast-feed or do not want to for whatever reason, realize that it does not have to affect your close connection to your babies, which is the most important consideration.

Setting personal infant-care goals based on your unique situation is the best guide to making decisions about how to feed your babies. One mother set a goal to breast-feed her twins for six months. She was firm in sticking to the babies' feeding schedule and persisted in following through with her commitment. Some of her friends and family were a bit dismayed by her "controlling" behavior surrounding her babies' feeding and sleep schedules, but she defended her decisions based upon her need to do what was best for her babies while still feeling in charge and competent.

Another new mother of twins expressed tremendous shame about her decision not to breast-feed her twins exclusively although she had planned to do so before their birth. She described how she tried to hide the bottle of formula in her diaper bag when she brought her twins to the pediatrician for their two-week checkup. Because she somehow felt she didn't have the right to make the infant-feeding decisions that worked best for her, she was very distressed when the nurse eyed the bottle in her bag and disapprovingly inquired why she was carrying formula!

Mothers of twins need to create their own standards whereby they accomplish what they can in the best way they can. And remember that strengthening the bond between you and each baby is what counts—with the breast or not.

Do You Need the Attention Your Twin Babies Attract?

After hearing a talk I had given to a parents-of-twins group, a mother came up to me and related how she now realized that she had used the attention her twin babies elicited in order to feed her own hunger for attention and admiration. She described how exhausted and depressed she had been in the initial months after the births and how she had made herself feel better by going out for walks with her twins so that she could receive "baby compliments" from passersby. Such positive attention helped to ameliorate the isolation and loneliness she felt caring for her babies all day. This young woman was open and insightful about the downside of her behavior, admitting that she had put her own need for validation above her babies' needs for alone time with her and separate experiences away from each other. But when the twins were about six months old, she discovered a solution for the need-for-attention problem. She hired a teenage babysitter in her neighborhood for a few hours every other day so that she could have some alone time with each baby. She related that she felt so positive about the benefits of spending time alone with each child that she regretted not having done so when the twins were younger. She told me that she was now happier and (somewhat) less exhausted—and was growing closer to each of her children.

It's virtually impossible to head out with a double stroller carrying two same-age babies without getting stopped by a steady stream of curious strangers. They may simply want to oooh and coo at your little ones, they may ask you stunningly personal questions, such as, "Were you on fertility drugs?" or they may want to engage you in a series of twinship queries and comments: "Are they identical?" "Who was born first?" "How do you tell them apart?" "Which one cries the loudest?" "How do you do it—you must be so exhausted!" The first few times you're bombarded with such questions, it's exciting, even flattering. After a while, perhaps your patience wears thin. But if you find yourself, like the woman I spoke with after my lecture, needing the attention your twins attract, you may want to think about where that need might come from. Are you receiving sufficient validation and appreciation from your spouse for all that you're doing? Are you using the baby compliments to try to compensate for how overwhelming parenting twin babies can be? Have you explored the possibility of getting more help with child care so that you can have more time to yourself, as well as more time to be alone with each child?

You deserve to be complimented on how adorable your children are, but, even more, you deserve adequate help, appreciation from your spouse, time alone with each baby, and time to replenish yourself. Also, getting loads of attention just for being twins is not the best thing for your babies anyway.

Babies and Siblings

How your older children react to their new twin brothers or sisters will depend on their age and how threatened they feel by the babies. Generally, the younger the sibling, the more likely he is to be upset by the new arrivals and to feel the need to compete for his parents' attention. Toddlers and preschoolers may have very real worries that you will abandon them now that your focus is on the babies. The older a child is, and the more secure he feels in relationship to his parents, the more apt he is to want to help with the care of the babies, play with the babies, and enjoy his big-brother role.

Regardless of their age, however, siblings are often thrown into an anxiety-ridden tailspin by the new babies. Dawn talked about how her four-year-old daughter, Kelly, reacted when her twin siblings were born.

> When I was pregnant, I assured Kelly that she was going to be my helper when the babies came. She seemed to love talking about the babies and was really looking forward to being their big sister. But in the chaos of these first four months, I think she has felt pushed into the background. She'll stand in the doorway to the babies' room while I'm feeding or changing one of them, and just kind of look at me in this forlorn way. It breaks my heart. I try to include her and carve out time for her, but I just don't have the time to spend with her like I used to. I know all of this is what has caused her bed-wetting, because she had never had an accident and had been toilet trained since she was two and a half.

Dawn and I talked about how it would be a good idea to routinely take Kelly out for a walk with just one baby so that she could act like the older sister rather than feel shut out by the attention her mom and others gave to the twins. Dawn made it a point to get help from a babysitter and from her husband so that there were opportunities for Kelly to accompany her and one baby on a walk or an errand. This strategy helped Kelly not only to reconnect with her mom but also to feel more like the big sister, rather than forlorn and inconsequential. Her bed-wetting behavior eventually stopped as she became more comfortable in her role as older sibling and made her adjustment to the twins.

Because twins demand lots of attention from their parents and attract a lot more of it from friends and strangers, it's easy for siblings to feel left out and unimportant. That's why taking a sibling and one baby for a separate outing is such a positive experience. Without the fuss that's constantly made over twin babies as a pair, the sibling can feel more involved with the new babies and even share some of the spotlight. For instance, if a friend or stranger stops to admire the baby, the older sibling will have the confidence to make the introduction. "This is my baby sister—and she's a twin!"

When I took our four-year-old daughter, Amy, to preschool with just one baby in tow, she would tell those who gathered around her wanting to see the baby that David was a twin. She was the important person who delivered the exciting news rather than someone relegated to the background, overshadowed by the spectacle of two babies. She had control over whether or not she even wanted to mention the twin issue. I also noticed that when Amy was in the car with only one baby, she engaged him, talked to him, and did so happily, whereas with two babies, she would often be cranky, act up, or complain— all attempts to gain my attention when there were two babies vying for it.

Since our other children were eight, six, and four when the twins were born, it was easier for them to be involved in helping us care for the babies. All three of our older kids were curious and intrigued with their baby brothers. And, like most babies, Jonny and David were fascinated by their older siblings. They smiled at them all the time and were eager to be part of their world. Jonny was so good natured as a baby that he didn't mind at all—in fact he loved it—when my older kids dressed him up in all kinds of wild costumes. They made him laugh, which was easy to do, and they also did their best to amuse David, who had a tough time initially but loved joining in the fun as he grew out of the colicky phase.

Although the twin mystique may claim that twin babies adore and need each other, in fact, babies are not that interested in other babies. They are, however, fascinated by older children. They love to watch them, listen to them, and learn from them. And older children know how to engage babies in a way that other babies (or adults) do not. So, once your older kids adjust to the competition and chaos that twins naturally usher in, be assured that they will have the opportunity to make two babies very happy.

Parents-of-Twins Journal: Babyhood

WRITE DOWN YOUR THOUGHTS

- What emotions have surfaced for you since you've been caring for your twins? Have you felt:

anxious	grateful	overwhelmed
delighted	blessed	guilty
disappointed	shocked	fulfilled

- Why do you think you've been experiencing these particular emotional states?
- How did the alone-time experiences with each baby make you feel? What did you discover about each child? About yourself?
- What are you looking forward to or worried about in the next stage of your babies' lives?

As you get clear on how parenting two babies is affecting you emotionally, remember that the more feelings you have, the better. Having access to a wide range of emotions, both positive and negative, allows you to be more fully alive. Being able to identify and articulate both the good and disturbing emotions you inevitably go through as a parent enables you to get through the more difficult stretches. Rather than feeling stuck or helpless, you'll be able to look forward to the next stage in your babies' lives with more confidence, curiosity, and enthusiasm.

Tips for Parents of Twin Babies

- Make sure that you provide each baby with separate experiences apart from his or her twin so that you have the chance to appreciate each as an individual.
- Don't compare one baby's milestone moments to the other's. Remember that each child develops at his or her own pace.
- Use your alone times with each baby to discover each child's unique personality.
- Don't feel guilty about preferring one baby's behavior over the other's. Your preferences don't mean that you

love one baby more than the other; rather, your preferences reveal your perception of each baby as a distinct being, which is always important to reinforce.

- Find a peer support group where you can openly discuss the parent-of-twins emotional overload you're likely experiencing.

• four •

FATHERS AND BABIES, FATHERS AND MOTHERS

With two babies, I've had the chance to take on a larger role, and I welcome that. But if I'm gonna take care of them, then my wife has to respect my way of doing things, which is really hard for her to do. I keep telling her there's more than one way to get a baby to go to sleep, but she seems to think my way is the absolute wrong way.

—RON, FATHER OF SIX–MONTH–OLD TWINS

An important benefit of having twins is the expanded opportunity for a father to be involved with his children when they're babies. A father's participation in early child care always enriches a child's life, but with twins it's a necessity. Moms don't just need help—they desperately need a coparent, even if they have a hard time admitting it. When twin babies are fortunate enough to have the active involvement of both parents, they don't have to struggle as much over sharing their mother, and they enjoy the added perk of getting to know their father more intimately from day one. Not only does dad's involvement lessen mom's burden and help lay the foundation for a stronger bond between father and each child, but it can also help to create a happier relationship between parents. Although conflicts can arise over everything from how best to get babies to sleep to how warmly they need to be dressed, sharing parenting responsibilities can ultimately make couples appreciate each other and bring them closer.

Nevertheless, there are issues that crop up between fathers and mothers of twins in the babyhood years, which are the focus of this chapter.

Can New Fathers of Twins Rescue New Mothers of Twins?

Even when fathers want to be involved in baby care, they are often met with their wives' baffling emotions. New moms of twins can be inexplicably angry toward their husbands, leaving them wondering what they did wrong and why they've been cast in the role of paternal villain. Fathers may be unaware that their wives feel out of sync with themselves, unable to connect with both babies, or guilty that they're unable to do it all. Overtired, overwhelmed, and resentful that they're missing out on the moments of blissful oneness between mother and child, new mothers of twins often take out their frustration on their husbands. Or a new mom may desperately look to her husband to supply the emotional fulfillment she's not receiving from the anticipated experience of motherhood. The bottom line is that it's common for a new mother of twins to long for her spouse to rescue her from all the new burdens she feels incapable of dealing with on her own. At the same time, however, she feels guilty for needing and wanting to be rescued.

So, where does that leave the new dad? In addition to feeling the economic pressure of having to provide for two new family members, men can feel profoundly confused by their wives' emotional swings. On the one hand, new moms are resentful that their spouses are not helping out more with the babies, and at the same time they're self-critical about needing the help. Many men may be unaware of a common female fantasy of motherhood in this earliest stage. This fantasy involves the romantic notion of mother satisfying all of baby's physical and emotional needs, baby making mother feel fulfilled and competent, and both inhabiting a self-contained universe in which no one else is needed. Many new mothers judge their maternal adequacy in terms of how well they can handle their parenting duties without any assistance. Needing assistance may engender feelings of dependency and helplessness, which can then lead to anger. So, it makes psychological sense that many new moms displace their self-criticism for feeling unable to manage two babies on their own by getting angry with their husbands.

While facing his wife's ambivalent maternal emotions, the typical new dad is going through his own emotional changes. He often feels disconnected from and abandoned by his wife and replaced by two tiny, needy babies whom he's trying his best to adjust to. He may attempt to help with child-care chores, even take on an equal parenting role, but his wife may be so critical of his efforts that he feels ineffectual or unappreciated. Added to all this is the common reality that the typical stressed-out new mother of twins is usually in no position to fulfill her husband's emotional or sexual needs adequately.

If you are a new father of twins, the best way to cope with your own stress and at the same time "rescue" your wife is to be as understanding, helpful, and gentle as you can. A new mom needs you to compliment her as often as possible on what a wonderful job she is doing. Tell her how fortunate you feel that she is the mother of your children. The slightest hint of disapproval or disdain can be construed as intensely critical or disparaging, especially in the initial months after your babies' arrival. On the other hand, the husband who walks into the house after work and says nothing about the mess or the lack of dinner on the table but empathetically asks how he can help—or simply takes charge of what obviously needs doing—will be rewarded with his wife's gratitude and tender feelings. Your positive, complimentary approach will help to diminish your wife's self-doubts and allow her to see you in a favorable light.

Of course, your own needs for affection and understanding are very important, but they may go unsatisfied until you and your wife begin to adjust to the tremendous changes two new babies usher in. Even though you are not experiencing the powerful physiological aspects of the birth and its aftermath, you, like you wife, are facing a vast new spectrum of emotions and pressures. So, it is necessary for fathers, as well, to take time for themselves. Perhaps a game of basketball, a jog, a massage, or an opportunity to watch a sporting event on television will be rejuvenating and enjoyable, a welcome respite from the seemingly never-ending baby routines. It also can be helpful to share your feelings with a sibling, a colleague, or a friend about this "new" parenting role. The camaraderie and support of other fathers is extremely valuable.

Marcela talked to me about how she had wanted her husband, Rudy, to rescue her in the early months after their twins were born. Unfortunately, she and Rudy had failed to talk to each other about how they both felt beaten down by the intense pressures of new parenthood. Marcela was struggling with the day-to-day chores of taking care of two babies, and although Rudy was a hardworking, caring person, he seemed to retreat into a world of his own after the twins were born. Their lack of communication finally caught up with them.

> I was so angry with my husband for the first three months after the twins were born. He would come home and tell me he had to take a hot bath before dinner, knowing full well that I hadn't had a moment to myself all day. After dinner, he would lie on the couch and never ask if there was anything he could do to help me. I was dying for him to offer to help feed the babies or put them to bed, but I figured if I had to ask, it wasn't worth it. I wondered why he couldn't see all that I was going through trying to take care of these two little babies by myself.
>
> One night he came home and all three of us were crying—both babies and me. He stood there sadly looking at us, me holding one of the twins, the other crying in her playpen, and then he sat down, put his head in his hands, and burst into tears, too, which really shocked me because Rudy never cries. Finally, he told me that he felt overwhelmed and helpless. He had planned to help me out with the babies in those first few months but was so exhausted at the end of the day now that he was working longer hours to earn more money. He also told me he missed the physical relationship between us, which had been nearly

nonexistent since the babies were born. I told him
how I had wanted to be rescued, for him to magically
take over the baby responsibilities when he got home.
I was at a breaking point—and so was he.

Marcela realized that she couldn't rely on something "magically" happening to turn things around. She and Rudy had to come up with a plan to save themselves and their relationship from falling apart. Although they couldn't afford to hire full-time help, they found a babysitter to help out from eight in the morning until two in the afternoon for a modest fee. This meant Marcela was less frazzled when Rudy came home from work, but she still needed his help in the evenings. Now that their respective needs were out in the open, Rudy was more responsive. He made it his job to feed one of the babies and put her to bed every night. He confided in Marcela that, in addition to being exhausted by his long hours at work, he had been intimidated by the prospect of caring for his infant daughters, worrying that he had no experience in baby care and might do something wrong. Marcela appreciated his frankness and was patient with Rudy as he learned the ropes. The help he provided not only strengthened Rudy's bond with his baby girls, but it also brought him and Marcela closer together.

In my experience, most new fathers of twins are well intentioned and loving. Like their spouses, they have undergone the emotional uncertainties surrounding a twin pregnancy and have joyfully anticipated the birth of their babies. Although financial worries and doubts about sharing their wife with two babies are often foremost in their minds, dads also look forward to the increased fathering opportunities that having twins provides. And when they take on a more active role in parenting their twins, sharing the challenges and joys of caring for two demanding babies, they are grateful for such a rewarding experience.

Even with the best intentions, however, when new parents of twins are feeling their way through the chaotic new world of never-ending parental chores and responsibilities, communication can get cut off or become emotionally charged. Husbands and wives who are able to express their feelings and opinions, as well as listen to one another and attempt to work out differences, have a greater chance of enjoying a harmonious relationship, even when two tiny newcomers enter the picture. As Marcela and Rudy discovered, being open with each other (even if it means breaking down in tears) is the first step.

A Dad's Way with Babies

As Ron's statement at the opening of this chapter makes clear, fathers and mothers can have conflicting ideas about how best to take care of their babies. Whether it's about feeding, burping, rocking, entertaining, or soothing, a difference of opinion over a relatively insignificant issue can give rise to marital tensions. Given that parents of twins need each other's good-humored participation in the myriad child-care tasks that need attention day in and day out, you'd think that each would allow the other to do it his or her way, as long as no one gets hurt, and the babies seem happy. But that's often not the case, and men especially seem to get flack for not attending to their babies in the "proper" way. Ron elaborated on the fireworks that erupted between him and his wife, Gina, over the issue of soothing baby Nicky to sleep.

Since Gina decided to bottle-feed both babies, it gives me the chance to fully participate in feeding them and putting them to sleep. We switch off with Sophie and Nicky so that they're each comfortable with both of us, and I think it all works out great. I grew up the oldest in a family of four kids, so I'm not fazed at all by babies—it's no big deal for me, and I enjoy it. The big deal is having to put up with Gina's narrow-mindedness. My way of putting Nicky to sleep is to give him his bottle while we watch the game or Everybody Loves Raymond *reruns. He's fine with it. I hold him, he watches, drinks his bottle, gets sleepy, and then I put him down. No problem. It doesn't work with Sophie; she prefers the lullaby CD Gina bought. So when it's my turn with her, that's what we do. But Gina somehow thinks I'm corrupting Nicky, that he'll grow up to be a TV addict. She's constantly yelling at me or walking off in a huff when she sees us in front of the tube. It's almost like she's jealous of our father-son bonding routine.*

I explained to Ron and Gina that couples often have different methods of caring for their babies, and that as long as the babies seem to be healthy and happy, there should be no need for one partner to censure the other's approach. Nicky seemed able to adapt to the "lullaby nights" with Gina, as well as to enjoy his daddy-and-me evenings in front of the small screen. And Ron acknowledged the pronounced differences between his twin babies by respecting Sophia's preference for the lullaby CD. As is often the case for some mothers, Gina may have been finding it hard to give up control over every aspect of her children's upbringing. Even in our post–women's lib era, a woman's sense of identity is still more closely tied to her parenting success than that of a man, which is why women often have a hard time giving up that parenting control and letting their husbands do things their way.

I often hear from my male clients that their wives become overly critical when they don't do things around the house or with the kids in the way that their wives deem correct. "She says she wants me to help out with the babies, and then when I do, she criticizes me for not doing things her way" is a common complaint from new dads. Unfortunately, mothers of twin babies are under so much pressure to accomplish a multitude of tasks, many of which are tedious and mind-numbing, that their nerves may be shot and their tolerance of a well-meaning dad's innovative parenting methods may be inappropriately low.

Again, my advice to fathers is first of all to try to be as gentle and understanding as possible. Acknowledge the stress your wife is under. Rather than come to verbal blows over whose bedtime ritual is best, gently remind your wife that your babies seem to be doing fine with mom's way of putting them to sleep as well as dad's. In fact, your twins will likely grow up to be that much more adaptable by having the opportunity to be parented by two distinct individuals.

Fear of Babies?

Unlike Ron, there are those men, like Rudy, who seem to be somewhat intimidated by babies. They love their children and look forward to caring for them when they get a little older but feel out of their league when they're around infants. "When babies are that small, they're so fragile that I'm afraid I'll do something wrong and put them at risk somehow," one new dad told me. Another mentioned that he felt it was a woman's job to handle infants, that it was a biological thing. "I'll get more involved with them when the babies are old enough to walk," he said.

Although such sentiments are more common than you might think, a new father's motives for leaving baby care to his wife can be misinterpreted. James is the proud father of three boys. After his wife, Darlene, gave birth to their twin sons, he informed her that he would take over the care of their five-year-old son but that the twins were to be her responsibility for the time being. Darlene had this to say:

> It was like he was handing down an executive order; he was cutting himself off from the twins while they were infants—and that was that. I was extremely upset and angry because I felt that I would be losing my older son, who would now belong exclusively to my husband. And I would be left on my own to take care of the babies, a job I couldn't possibly handle alone. It felt like we were dividing up into two families: James and our older son, and me and the babies. I was also confused because James had been such a supportive partner during the whole infertility-treatment process. It was the two of us going through this thing together, which happily led to the twins' birth. So, how could he now not want anything to do with them?

I explained to Darlene that, after their wives give birth, men often feel abandoned by them, and when there are two babies, a man's sense of displacement can be even greater. James's "edict" had little to do with not loving or wanting the babies and much to do with his own fear of abandonment. The new babies required so much attention and care that there was rarely any stress-free time left for Darlene and James to enjoy each other's company. In response to feeling the loss of his wife's attention, James seemed to be bowing out entirely from caring for the twins until the infant phase was over.

But there was another motive for James's pronouncement. His declaration that he would leave the babies to Darlene and take full responsibility for their older son, although stated undiplomatically, was actually his way of demonstrating that he wanted to be as helpful as possible. He thought he would be doing Darlene a big favor by lessening her child-care load. Realizing that she needed a great deal of help taking care of three children, he assumed that by his taking charge of their five-year-old, Darlene would feel greatly relieved. Of course, she didn't react that way at all. From Darlene's perspective, not only was James shirking his responsibility as the father of their babies, but he was depriving her of time with their older son.

Once Darlene and I discussed these issues, she understood more clearly how the twins' arrival was affecting James and how his intentions were essentially good ones. She came to empathize with him as he struggled to adjust to being temporarily displaced by two babies. She told him how much she valued and appreciated the loving care he was providing for their eldest son. And she managed to communicate to him, without anger, that his help was sorely needed with the twins as well, that she needed him, and the babies did, too. Within a short time, James forgot about his "executive order" and willingly joined Darlene in caring for the babies.

Father-and-Baby Alone Time

Whether dad takes one baby at a time for a walk in the single stroller or to do an errand or just spends time alone with his new son or daughter in another room of the house, both he and the baby will benefit in numerous ways. Fathers tend to have a different style of relating to babies than mothers do—they're often more playful, more adventurous, and more flexible—and this way of interacting is a good experience for babies to have. Each child benefits from father-and-baby alone time in order to foster a close bond. Being able to experience dad's style and energy allows each baby to learn about the world from a new perspective.

Dennis shared with me how much fun he had with each of his twin daughters, Emily and Grace. Although the girls hadn't yet reached their first birthday, Dennis had already learned about their individual personalities, likes, and dislikes. And each daughter was learning about dad and herself through her distinct alone-time adventures. Dennis explained how his and his wife's parenting styles differed.

> My wife is a wonderful mom, but she has more of the "you-gotta-be-prepared-for-every-emergency" orientation than I do. Before she takes one of the girls out for a walk, she has to make sure she's got the diaper bag and the bottle and the Cheerios and the toys and all the other things they might need "just in case." I'm much more spontaneous; I'm not afraid to just grab one of my daughters and head out the door. If I have to wait until we get home to change a diaper, it's not a major problem. What's more important is knowing what each of them likes to do, and it's been a trial-and-error deal.

I found out recently that Emily loves it when I put her in the stroller and we walk over to Petco and look at the fish and the birds. The look that comes over her face when the parakeets chirp and fly around and do their thing is priceless. She's also fascinated by all the colorful tropical fish and can sit there a long time watching them swim around. Grace hates sitting in the stroller for very long—doesn't like to be confined. So, usually we'll just go outside in the backyard, and I let her crawl around on the grass. She likes to pull up fistfuls of grass, look for bugs, stuff like that. Sometimes I'll get down on the grass with her, and we'll roll her big rubber ball back and forth. She may get grass stained and dirty, which my wife doesn't always love, but Grace loves the outdoors. I can already imagine her kicking a soccer ball or stealing bases one day.

Babies like Grace and Emily are lucky to have an enthusiastic, involved dad like Dennis, someone who obviously relishes his role as a parent. Babies' separate alone times with their fathers will teach them about themselves in ways that don't necessarily come out when they're with their mom. It's also good when parents, like Dennis and his wife, are tolerant of each other's unique parenting styles because their babies are exposed to different ways of interacting with people and their environment. Also, the bond each establishes with her father at this early stage in life will likely be stronger thanks to the dad's attentive focus on each baby's unique personality.

As you consider how you might spend alone time with each of your babies, keep in mind what Dennis discovered with Emily and Grace. Experiment. See what each one responds to positively, what brings smiles or looks of fascination. What engrosses one baby (watching fish swim by in a pet-store tank) may bore the other. Pulling up fistfuls of grass isn't every baby's idea of time well spent, but hanging out one-on-one with a patient, attentive dad definitely is.

Meeting Your Wife's Expectations: An Impossible Mission?

An unexpected challenge for many new fathers of twins is a woman's prenatal fantasy of how her husband will respond to the babies' arrival. I've discovered that many women have an idealized vision of the perfect new father, and while this may run counter to the actual husband's personality, new moms still hope their mate might somehow fulfill this fantasy. Hopeful women imagine how this sensitive, fatherly Prince Charming will respond to his wife as a new mother of twins, how perfectly attentive and helpful he'll be, how he'll know exactly what to do to make mother and babies happy and comfortable. But once the babies are born and moms start feeling overwhelmed, inadequate, or both, they can feel profoundly disappointed in their husbands. After all, how many men can possibly live up to the Charming New Father fantasy?

Women in my groups have mentioned these reasons for being disappointed in their husbands:

- "I want him to rescue me at the end of another harrowing day—and he doesn't know how!"
- "I want him to tell me, 'You're such a wonderful mother. This must be so hard on you. I don't know how you do

it, sweetheart!'—and instead he complains about the messy house!"

- "He needs me to tell him what to do! Isn't it obvious, with two crying babies, no dinner on the table, and four baskets of dirty laundry?"

For their part, new dads are often frustrated that their wives don't cut them any slack. They tell me,

- "I offer to help, but it's like I can't do anything right. Whatever I do, it's not enough!"
- "She doesn't understand that I work hard during the day, too, and am exhausted when I come home. I'm willing to help out, but don't I deserve a rest first?"
- "I feel like I've gained two helpless little creatures and lost a wife. She not only doesn't have time for me, she has little interest in me. It's all about the babies, even when we manage to sneak out for an hour to ourselves."

While most new parents encounter unfamiliar difficulties, parents of twins face at least double the challenges. The physical stress is compounded, and the emotional upheaval is greatly intensified. Many of the moms in my twins group who had a single child prior to having their twins reported that in comparison they had felt less irritated with their husbands after their singleton was born. However, the birth of twins for these experienced moms was filled with unanticipated feelings. "I feel like my life is spinning out of control," is a common refrain for mothers of twins, whether or not they've had children before.

How does a well-meaning father deal with a "spinning-out-of-control" wife who also may be harboring a hidden resentment against him for not matching up to her fantasy superdad?

If, as a dad, you're truly invested in taking care of your babies, not only will you be forging a strong bond with your children, but by sharing the baby-care burden, you'll become, if not a super-hero, at least a superappreciated husband. Initially, however, you may not feel appreciated at all. Often dads feel that their wives criticize them over the smallest infractions. "She wants it done her way or else," is a constant complaint. One new dad I counseled protested that his wife chastised him for changing his clothes first thing when he got home from work, rather than heading directly to check on the babies. Another reported that his wife scolded him for pouring himself a cup of coffee in the morning before feeding the babies: "She's got a schedule with the babies, and if I don't follow it to the T, she goes ballistic."

I generally advise men with such grievances to hang in there; the criticism will likely diminish once women begin to adjust to the "twin babies overload." When your wife's frantic moods subside (and they will), she'll be able to relate to you more fully. And she'll be deeply grateful to you, your tolerance, and the invisible white horse you rode in on.

New mothers of twins most want to hear the following messages from their husbands. When new dads convey these thoughts to their wives, both parents will likely enjoy a more comfortable adjustment to their two new babies.

NEW DADS, TELL YOUR WIFE . . .

- "You're doing a great job!"
- "Being a mom to two babies is so difficult and taxing. You need some time for yourself. How can I help?"
- "How do you manage to accomplish so much when the babies are so demanding?"

- "Don't worry if you didn't have time to cook or straighten up. I can see that you are handling as much as possible."
- "Let's make a date to go out together, as soon as you feel up to it!"
- "You are not going crazy. I promise things will get better little by little."
- "Don't feel guilty for complaining. It's good to get things off your chest. And remember that you're a terrific mom!"

He's My Hero:
My Experience

When our three older singleton children were born, my husband was involved and helpful in a variety of ways, but I was pretty much in charge. I think he felt a bit out of the loop because breast-feeding each infant made them more attached to me in the beginning. When Jonny and David came along, and I realized that I couldn't handle them on my own, Robert pitched in and became my greatest ally. Since both babies were bottle-fed, David exclusively and Jonny intermittently, Robert shared the ongoing responsibility of feeding them, which fostered his close connection to the boys right away. He would sit in our rocking chair holding one baby or the other in his arms, sometimes talking to him, sometimes humming, and those early one-on-one experiences couldn't help but draw father and sons closer.

Robert had experience with three babies prior to the birth of our twins, so he knew that burping and changing generally followed feeding and that a crying baby is not something to fear. But even first-time dads can learn to anticipate the needs of their babies with a little practice. It doesn't take long before a new parent discovers what a baby's cry signifies, how each baby responds to you, and what will best soothe him when he's cranky. We had our share of difficulties as we adjusted to caring for Jonny and David. Like most couples, we had disagreements that escalated amid bouts of frustration, fatigue, and frantic impatience. Since I needed Robert's involvement with both babies right from the start, I appreciated that he wanted to help feed, change, bathe, and spend time with them in their first year of life. He knew that I needed him to coparent our baby boys, and he appreciated being needed. Having the chance to bond with his sons early on deepened his relationship with each of them and gave new meaning to his concept of fathering.

Unlike me, who worried about David's constant crying and wondered if I were an inadequate mom for being unable to soothe him, Robert optimistically assured me that the colic would subside and that David would be just fine once it did. I found his attitude wonderfully calming. Of course, even pros have their questionable moments—like the evening I had left the babies with Robert and came home to find him dozing on the floor, with both boys happily crawling around on the living room rug, wired from their late-night coffee ice cream snack with Dad.

Parents-of-Twins Journal: Fathers and Babies, Fathers and Mothers

DADS, WRITE DOWN YOUR THOUGHTS

- How do you feel about being needed to coparent your two babies?
- What problems have developed between you and your wife since the birth of your babies?

- What do you most enjoy about being with each of your babies? What do you find most difficult?
- How do you think the early involvement with your twins will affect your relationship with each of them later on?

MOMS, WRITE DOWN YOUR THOUGHTS

- What was your prenatal fantasy about how your husband would treat you and your babies? How does that differ from reality?
- How do you feel about the level of involvement your husband has with the babies?
- What problems have developed between you and your husband since the birth of your babies?
- How do you both show your appreciation for each other, for all that you're doing as parents of twins?

Tips for Fathers of Twin Babies

- Be as involved as possible from the beginning of your babies' lives. This will help you establish your role as a father, ease your wife's desperation, and, most importantly, help to form a unique relationship with each baby from day one. Babyhood is a wonderful time to begin to know each child as a single being, apart from his twin and his mother.
- Help your wife spend alone time with each baby by spending your own alone time with the other child. This way you'll both feel uniquely connected to each child. You might want to establish a routine whereby you take

turns taking walks, doing errands, or just hanging out with one baby at a time.

- Make your own plans for alone time with each baby, choosing activities you and each child enjoy. This way, you won't feel as if you're being controlled by your wife or on the receiving end of her directives.

- Let your wife know that you are supportive of her getting the outside help she may need. New moms tend to be hard on themselves and may view the need for help as a measure of their own inadequacy. Help your wife understand that this is definitely not the case.

- Make time to be together with your wife—just the two of you. With all that you're both going through, you need experiences that help you reconnect and enjoy each other's company away from your babies.

- Think about reconnecting primarily with physical affection rather than sexual contact in the initial period after the babies' births. With patience and empathy, this will undoubtedly lead to greater intimacy.

- When your wife reveals how distraught she is by all that is expected of her as a new mother of twins, don't feel you need to come up with specific solutions. She will appreciate just being listened to. Your empathic approach will be vital to developing a healthy relationship with your children as well.

- Understand that the greatest gift you can give your wife is your time, patience, and love.

five

THE PRESCHOOL YEARS

During a recent Saturday trip to the mall with my daughters, I felt pulled in two opposite directions. Molly saw a group of kids in the play area at the food court and ran ahead to join them. I thought it was a good sign that she wanted to play with the other kids since she's only recently begun to socialize at preschool. But Rena started crying, "Don't go, Molly! I don't want you to go there!" I hated to see Rena so upset and wondered if I should just tell Molly no. But I didn't want to hold her back. So, who do I take care of? If I let Molly go, Rena will continue her fit, and if I don't let Molly go, I'll be thwarting her healthy independence!

I had to make a quick decision, and I decided to let Molly go play with the other kids while Rena and I sat close by and had some pizza. Rena was still upset, mad at her sister for abandoning her, but I think I instinctively knew I had done the right thing.

—BRET, FATHER OF THREE-YEAR-OLD DAUGHTERS

Parents of twins are usually so overwhelmed during the first few years of their children's lives that the preschool years seem like a welcome respite. Moms and dads no longer have to juggle an endless cycle of feeding, changing, soothing, and putting to bed two helpless babies. Instead, they're delighted when their toddlers begin to develop their language skills, feed themselves, learn to use the potty, and enjoy a bit more independence. They're learning what it's like to make friends outside the family. Enjoying their mobility and new cognitive abilities, they demonstrate a wonderful curiosity about the world and the people in it. Some twins at this age easily become each other's natural playmate, which can be helpful to stressed-out parents, who desperately need a little time to themselves.

So, is this preschool-age twin togetherness a good thing? And how can parents like Bret respond when the togetherness is threatened? In this chapter, we'll consider the pros and cons of twin togetherness, as well as how to handle twins' inevitable developmental differences as they grow from toddlers to kindergarteners. We'll also discover why parents of twins may teach a different lesson when it comes to "sharing" and why preschool-age twins' "caretaking" behavior can have some limiting consequences.

Too Much Togetherness?

As we mentioned in chapter 3, many twins begin to interact with each other around six to ten months of age. As same-age siblings begin to discover one another, it's a thrill for parents to watch as the two hug, play, and communicate. Even their sibling squabbles are fascinating to parents who are learning to discern each child's unique personality. Most enthralling to parents of twins, however, is the ease with which each twin seems to anticipate the other's needs.

One mom told me she reveled in the fact that her two-year-old son brought his brother the pacifier whenever he was upset. Another mother spoke about how her three-year-old daughter hugged her sister whenever she was distraught. While parents of singletons complain that their preschoolers often have a hard time learning to share their toys with other kids, several parents of twins seem to have a special story about how easily the two share their belongings and how one child seems to look after the other. It's not that preschool-age twins never fight or argue, but parents are understandably impressed with their twins' compassion toward each other and their overall ability to get along. When it comes to their twin relationship, they seem to have interpersonal skills that singletons of the same age simply don't have.

With this in mind, many parents of preschool-age twins relate that twinship has some sweet benefits that make up for the initial rough ride. Parents rightfully brag about how the twins take care of one another, share their possessions, and play with each other for long periods, thus freeing up mom and dad to have a bit of time to themselves. While parents of singletons must become their child's social secretary, scheduling playdates and classes in order to afford their youngster the chance to be around other kids, parents of twins consider themselves lucky to be freed from making such arrangements. The twins have each other. But is there such a thing as too much togetherness at this stage in your children's development?

Given that twins appear to enjoy being with one another, what's the harm in their spending most of their time together? Since twin togetherness is taken for granted as an inherent piece of the twin relationship, it may not occur to you that your twins might be missing an important part of their social and emotional education by not having the experiences singletons have. When they cling to the safety net of their automatic friendship with their twin, many children have difficulty forming relationships and making friends outside the family. In identifying so closely with their twin, they can come to feel that they must always act according to the needs of the couple, rather than their own needs. If twins go through their childhood as a couple, they miss out on experiencing their individuality as they interact with other people.

Perhaps you're wondering, isn't considering her twin's needs a good thing? Won't the constant attention to each other's feelings teach my twin children compassion when they get older? The problem is that twin relationships involving too much togetherness might push compassion into the unhealthy realm of negating one's own abilities, desires, and goals. Peter and Joshua are a case in point.

Doreen consulted with me regarding a preschool situation with her four-year-old fraternal twin boys. Peter had speech problems due to a congenital birth defect, and his brother, Joshua, who had no speech difficulties, had "joined" in Peter's problem by refusing to speak to anyone except Peter at pre-school. The boys' preschool teacher was alarmed by the brothers' inability or unwillingness to interact with the other children in class. Their special status as an incommunicative duo cut off from the rest of the group precluded any other friendships or acquaintances.

How had the boys' family history contributed to their preschool standoff? Peter and Josh were the third and fourth children in a family with two older siblings. Doreen had tried her best to be attentive to all of her children but understandably found herself spread thin. As parents of twins so often do, she described how wonderful it was that her twin sons entertained one another as this provided some relief in her hectic schedule. Also, their close relationship seemed to enhance Doreen's maternal pride in being a mother of twins. She had obviously done something right to enable these two little guys to get along so well. But the preschool problem, especially Josh's decision to "share" his brother's silence, forced Doreen to explore the possible pitfalls inherent in a too-close twin relationship.

Doreen was initially surprised and angered by my suggestion that too much togetherness might have contributed to her sons' present situation. She told me that she felt criticized and misunderstood, and she staunchly defended the fact that her sons were best friends with a special, loving connection. She was upset that I had dared to question a relationship that was "so special and dear." As we talked further, however, she began to understand how the boys' exclusive relationship created a barrier to their self-discovery, as well as to other friendships and each boy's relationship to Doreen and her husband. She came to realize how a lack of psychological boundaries between twin children can lead to confused roles and inappropriate behavior. What she initially thought of as cute, loving, devoted twin behavior was turning into an us-against-them situation in which her boys had become a hostile, defiant couple who refused to socialize with others in an age-appropriate manner.

In the course of our sessions together, Doreen shared her feelings of guilt and resentment about the boys' twinship. She described how out of control she had felt when they were born. She had tried to establish an intimacy with each one but felt frustrated and overwhelmed by their needs. Exhausted and re-sentful that the boys' demands interfered with her attentiveness to her other children, she felt increasingly disconnected from them. She told me, "I never got a handle on things because I felt constantly discombobulated and annoyed by two babies needing me at the same time."

Doreen hoped to bury these shameful feelings and bask in the glow of the idealized twinship. As the boys approached their first birthday, she began to marvel at how they became so in-volved with each other. She failed to recognize how she had opted out of the picture and backed away from involving herself with either of them as separate people. It did not occur to her to be alone with each baby or to provide either of them with different experiences. Looking back, Doreen realized that she had bought into the twin mystique as a way to assuage her guilt and re-morse. "I figured they were happiest just being together. . . . In a way, they didn't really need me."

Various child-development experts agree that a parent must parent a child; a child cannot parent another child. However, in so many instances, twins are left to parent one another because their parents misunderstand the twin relationship. Being twins is an opportunity to have a close sibling relationship with someone your own age, but it does not take the place of being nurtured and guided by your parents. Time spent playing with your twin is not a substitute for one-on-one time with mom or dad. Nor does it offer the same opportunity for developmental growth as making new friends—at the park, in a class, or at preschool. A healthy twinship evolves when each sibling goes through the process of developing an individuated self. Parents need to en-courage this process by spending alone time with each child and providing each twin with enough opportunities to be separate from the other.

Wanting to Be Her Own Person

While it may not seem like an earthshaking event, Molly's three-year-old desire to break away from her sister and father and go off to join the play group at the mall was a major step—and an age-appropriate one. Although Bret felt torn because his other daughter, Rena, was upset by Molly's determination to go play with the kids, he clearly did the right thing by allowing Molly to reach out to other children. It may be that Rena had become too dependent on her twin sister to fulfill her social needs, or perhaps Bret and his wife had not considered the importance of providing the girls with sufficient opportunities to have separate activities and playdates, which contributed to Rena's panic about being with other kids without her sister as a partner. Or maybe Rena was simply a less outgoing individual at this stage in her young life, which is a difference to be respected. Bret instinctively realized at the mall, however, that Molly was on the right track; the preschool years are the appropriate time to begin to branch out and make decisions on one's own. At this age, a young child begins to become her own advocate, making choices about what she wants and statements about how she feels. While challenging for parents, children are supposed to do this at this age—challenge their parents in order to test the boundaries between what they desire and what parents will allow.

For parents of twins, preschooler independence is complicated by additional issues, as Molly and Rena's story reveals. First of all, there is the practical consideration of a parent's inability to be in two places at once. Bret and Rena had to stay close to the play area at the mall in order for Bret to keep an eye on Molly. Had he and Molly been alone, just the two of them, Bret wouldn't have had to deal with Rena's negative reaction. This is a good argument for preschooler "alone time" with mom or dad: each child will have the opportunity to explore on her own without the influence of the other twin, and mom or dad won't have to juggle the supervision of two preschoolers who want to go off in two different directions.

Then there is the emotional interplay between the two siblings. What if one child is ready to strike out on her own, and the other isn't? Or what if one habitually shadows the other, thereby preventing the more independent twin from doing her own thing? Again, one solution is alone time with mom or dad so that neither twin will be unduly influenced by her sibling and will be free to develop her own preferences and ideas. Another is separate activities with other children, which we'll talk about further later on in the chapter.

The important thing to keep in mind is that, at this stage in the lives of your twins, each child needs you to recognize her separate sense of self. By imposing her will on you and her sibling, she is attempting to define her individuality. Wanting more control over her own actions is the beginning of each twin's journey toward selfhood. At the same time, knowing how much decision-making power to give over to a preschooler is a difficult transition for every parent. And when there are two preschoolers, the question of who has control over whom makes the transition even more demanding. So be prepared for power struggles—times two.

What to wear, a seemingly innocuous issue, is cause for some typical parent-preschooler power plays. When our children are babies, we get used to dressing them according to what we determine is most comfortable and appropriate, based on their age, the weather, and what pleases us sentimentally or aesthetically. We change their diapers, dress them warmly if it's cold outside, and choose that cute pale-green jacket that matches her eyes or the bright red sweatshirt that he looks so adorable in. Then, in what seems like a flash, our maturing toddlers begin to interfere with our decisions and turn what used to be a simple routine into an ordeal. She throws down the green jacket and insists on wearing only her glittery T-shirt. Her twin brother, who had been happy in his sweatshirt, sees his sister protesting mom's fashion choice and follows suit by tossing the red garment into the trash. Clearly, both twins are attempting to assert their independence, and that's a good thing. But what's a mom to do when one two-year-old wants to wear a T-shirt in 40 degree weather, and the other wants to go out in his pajama top?

Offering a choice of two items and allowing each toddler to make his or her own decision—in this case, "Here are two shirts. Choose the one you like. And here are two jackets. Choose the one that you want to wear"—honors the need of each for self-assertion and control without instigating a battle over dressing. It is important for the twins to have the opportunity to make their own choices without the influence of you or their same-age sibling.

As your twins develop from two to five years old, they'll likely reveal their need for individuality in various ways. Amanda was taken aback by her three-and-a-half-year-old son's demonstrated need for individuality and separation from his twin brother.

> *I'm a little embarrassed about admitting it now, but I was really upset when Dylan came to me and insisted on having his own dresser drawers. He didn't want his clothes to be "mixed together," as he put it, with his brother's. I was convinced that Dylan's wanting to be separate from Alex would be the beginning of a whole slew of changes that I was terrified of. What if I had to start moving furniture around in their room? And was I now going to be forced to label all their clothing? Why couldn't Dylan just accept that I had a certain system that worked for me? I know it sounds ridiculous that I worried so much about such a small thing, but it didn't seem small at the time. Now I've learned more about why it was a healthy sign that Dylan wanted to keep his things separate from Alex's.*

Amanda feared Dylan's wishes for a modest sense of individuality not simply because she would have to reorganize the boys' room and label their clothes. She also feared that Dylan's wish for separateness threatened her own connection to the twins, as well as her identity as a mother of twins. Her sense of equilibrium and control was disrupted by what she rightly knew to be the burgeoning individuation of her twin sons, and she responded with anxiety and panic. In fact, Dylan was merely expressing a preschooler's developmental need for individuality and personal space. Interestingly, his brother, Alex, adapted to the changes in the bedroom—with each boy having two drawers to himself—much more easily than Amanda did. "I like having my own drawers and my own clothes, Mom!" he told her.

Amanda realized that she had to come to terms with the fact that her sons' lives couldn't be managed solely according to what was easiest or most comfortable for her. Part of her role as parent to her twins was to provide each boy with opportunities to experience himself as separate from his same-age sibling, including the opportunity to keep his very own shirts and socks in his very own separate drawer.

Teaching Twins Not to Share

According to clinical psychologist Barbara Shave Klein, twins are inherently predisposed to sharing from the time of conception. They share space in the womb, precious time with their parents, and usually a bedroom. One of our responsibilities as parents of twins, however, is to help our preschool-age children realize that they don't have to share everything with their same-age sibling. Just like singletons, they are entitled to their own time with mom or dad, their own friends, their own experiences, and their own things. Since twins are called upon to share everything from their toys to their parents' attention, it is important for twins to learn not to share all the time. In fact, too much required sharing between same-age siblings can interfere with each child's ability to develop an individuated self. Feeling entitled to what is theirs and theirs alone helps children gain a sense of their individual place in the world. Singletons take this proprietary sense for granted, and as parents of twins, we need to provide our children with opportunities to experience this feeling of ownership as well.

With this in mind, make sure that your preschool-age twins have their own personal items, just like singleton siblings, such as different sweatshirts, pajamas, shoes, and jackets, all of which you can label with their names. If they want to wear each other's things or share each other's toys, that is up to them. And, of course, there will be certain larger items—a train set, a toy stove, a rocking horse—that they will inevitably share; you certainly can't be expected to buy two of everything. Other than these big-ticket items, however, make it clear to your children that what belongs to one does not belong to the other. Again, adhering to boundaries about what belongs to whom promotes a needed sense of ownership and individuality.

Not being required to share everything with their same-age sibling doesn't mean that your twins don't need to share with other children when they're at preschool or on a playdate. Learning to share with other kids is one of the key lessons of preschool socializing, and chances are your twins will find this easier than many of their singleton classmates.

I'm Not My Brother's Keeper

An offshoot of too much twin togetherness is the twin caretaking pattern, which many parents of twins witness in their young children. This can happen when one twin is more self-assured, outgoing, domineering, or perhaps stronger physically than the other, or it can occur when one child is physically or mentally challenged, and the other is not. It may seem natural, cute, and loving when one twin takes care of the other. But it's important to understand that when the roles of caretaker and cared-for twin become inflexible, each child's capacity to express his multifaceted personality is diminished.

So, how do we help our children to play well together and be considerate of one another without crossing the line into the caretaking syndrome? The first step is to become aware of a pattern your twins could be falling into. Perhaps you identify with one of these caretaking scenarios:

- Two-and-a-half-year-old Marcie moves around easily while her twin sister, Josie, struggles with her sense of balance due to a physical handicap. Marcie lovingly brings Josie the toy that she is struggling to grab but then trips her on purpose as she walks by.

- At a birthday party, outgoing three-year-old Samantha brings her shy twin brother, Michael, some birthday cake. She happily answers for Michael when other kids or grown-ups ask him a question. At home, Samantha takes it upon herself to ask Michael what toy he wants to play with or what snacks he wants, and then she gets those for him. She looks forward to the praise her mother often gives her for "being so helpful to your brother."

- Four-year-old twin brothers Andrew and Danny have always enjoyed playing together at home. Danny is the caretaking twin who soothes Andrew when he gets upset or offers to give him the toy he's playing with so Andrew won't get jealous. Lately, however, Danny has begun to sneak off and go under his bed with a flashlight to look at a book on his own. Andrew feels lost, upset, and angry when this happens and rushes to his mom to enlist her help in finding Danny.

In each of these instances, the caretaking twin either acts out displeasure at being expected to look after his or her sibling or anticipates praise for being such a good Samaritan. When he goes off to look at a book under his bed, Danny is seeking some private space away from his dependent twin brother. Marcie seems happy enough helping her sister do things that come easily for Marcie but later expresses resentment by tripping her physically challenged twin. And Samantha expects that her mother will love her more or think of her as better than her twin brother because she's doing for him what Michael can't seem to do for himself. Are each of these sets of twins locked in the caretaking mold—or is there a way out?

Singletons learn to cope with life's challenges as individuals, and twins, as well, need to develop their own problem-solving skills. If one twin is accustomed to having his same-age sibling help him navigate developmental tasks, he might be unprepared to approach the next rung on the ladder toward independence by himself. As for the caretaker, if he doesn't begin to carve out an individual path for himself, as Danny is beginning to do, he, too, will become dependent. He very likely will depend on being the dominant figure or caretaker in future relationships.

As parents, it can be heart wrenching to watch as one twin pines for the other, who is off by himself reading a book, or as the shy child adjusts to being without his gregarious twin at a birthday party. It's natural for siblings who are close friends to miss each other when they're apart. But it's important to realize that there is an essential difference between missing one's twin and needing him. When twins are overly reliant on each other, that need is unhealthy. Due to the twin mystique, you may assume that same-age siblings won't be able to tolerate being separated, but they can learn to get along on their own in the same way that singleton children do. Singleton or twin, a young child can learn to cope with the anxiety of being on his own in a new situation away from the predictability of his family. In fact, doing so is part of his developmental "homework," and unless he completes it, he may struggle to graduate to the next stage of childhood.

More often than not, a child's anxiety will dissipate eventually as he soothes himself through the adjustment to new people and a new environment. It is important for each twin to have the opportunity to develop his own coping strategies. Otherwise, he is deprived of an important step toward independence. The caretaker must provide the other twin with guidance and support as well so he will learn that he does not have to be the dominant person or caretaker in all future relationships. Let's see how the parents of each set of twins dealt with their children's caretaking patterns.

- Marcie and Josie's dad noticed that Marcie would help her sister with a particular task, then later undermine her, as she had when she tripped her. During an alone-time afternoon together, dad talked to Marcie about Josie's need to begin to do things for herself, telling Marcie, "She'll never learn if you keep doing it for her." He also talked to his wife about getting Marcie enrolled in a morning preschool class so that she could make friends with children who were at her developmental level. Josie would join a class when she was ready.

- A neighborhood child said to Samantha and Michael's mom, "Samantha always talks for Michael. Is Michael afraid of us?" This comment made her recognize that an unhealthy dynamic had developed between the twins. As a result, she made it a point to tell Samantha not to answer for Michael, to let him speak for himself. And she realized that she needed to arrange separate play-dates for each of them so that Michael would learn to interact with children on his own, and Samantha would be free to break away from her caretaking role.

- Danny and Andrew's parents discussed Danny's new habit of retreating under his bed and understood that he needed time to himself. They told him it was fine that he go under the bed to look at his books, but if he wanted privacy, all he had to do was tell Andrew he wanted to be alone for a while. Mom and dad would make sure that Andrew didn't disturb his private time. They also zeroed in on Andrew's interests, particularly those activities he might be able to do on his own, like working on his animal puzzles. Realizing that he would whine for Danny at first, they nonetheless encouraged Andrew to use his private time to do what he enjoyed most.

Separate and Fun:
Playdates and Other Activities

Five-year-old Aidan begged his parents to let him join a T-ball program, but his twin brother, Justin, had no interest in that sport. Their father, Wayne, reacted to this difference between the boys as if it signified the breakup of the family. He felt guilty, as if Justin were being left behind. He tried to pressure the boys to choose a joint activity. Instead of welcoming their separate interests, Wayne feared that their solo activities would disrupt the family's unity. Up to this point, the boys had pretty much done everything together. They were in the same preschool group and were each other's playmates at home. When they had friends over, they both played with the same playmate or playmates. But, instead of valuing Aidan's expression of separateness, Wayne believed that Aidan's solo ball games would hurt Justin and the family.

In fact, Justin adjusted very well to the T-ball separations, which gave him the chance to play with some of his favorite toys uninterrupted by his brother. It was Wayne who had difficulty adjusting to the new routine, and it seems his adjustment went deeper than getting over his guilty feelings about leaving Justin at home. He was sad and disappointed by what he called the "breakup" because, as he told me, "My vision of the twins' lives together was being negated. All of a sudden, they were going off on their own in separate directions." Wayne then disclosed that, as an only child, he had always longed for a brother, someone who would share all the fun times of childhood. Being on the same sports team with a brother would have been his dream come true.

It took some time before Wayne's emotional response to the "breakup" was tempered by his reasoned understanding that the opportunity to choose and enjoy separate activities promoted positive development and constituted an essential part of growing up. Aidan loved the camaraderie of being on a sports team, and Justin enjoyed the time alone to play with his action figures. Wayne realized that he had to work through his disappointment about the twin mystique not ringing true in his family. Once he saw that Aidan and Justin were flourishing in their separate activities, he let go of the fantasy that twins need to stick together through playtime, sports time, and free time.

If your twins are still babies, and you decide to follow the parenting philosophy I've presented so far, you won't have the dilemma that Wayne had. Your twins will be introduced to separate activities from babyhood, and when they're old enough for T-ball or guitar lessons or preschool, they will adjust smoothly to the experience of making their own friends and doing things on their own, apart from their same-age sibling. If this new way to bring up twins as separate individuals has been your guideline, you won't have those nagging feelings of guilt and remorse about "breaking up" your children.

On the other hand, if your twins have never been separated, they may go through a challenging transition when you introduce the idea of separate activities at this stage. Unlike Justin, some preschool-age children initially have a hard time being "left behind" while their twin enjoys a separate activity. As a parent, you might feel badly for the child whose turn to do his own thing hasn't come around yet. But this is an opportunity to talk to your children about having fun doing what interests them and being with friends apart from their twin. Your conversation with your preschool-age child might go something like this:

> YOU: So, you know that your brother is starting a gym class tomorrow, right?
> YOUR CHILD: I don't like somersaults and trampoline!

YOU: I know you don't. And that's why he's taking the class
and you're not.

YOUR CHILD: But what will I do while he's at the class?

YOU: Grandma will come and stay with you, and I'm sure
the two of you will have fun together. Maybe bake
some cookies.

YOUR CHILD: That's not fair! I have to have a babysitter, and
he doesn't!

YOU: But once a week you'll get a chance to choose something you like to do—maybe a music class or a run at the
beach with me or Daddy. So think about what you'd
have fun doing, okay?

YOUR CHILD: What about my brother?

YOU: That will be his time to stay with Grandma.

Taking turns engaging in separate activities is a great way to
make sure that both children have a chance to explore something
they enjoy doing. Of course, there will be instances when
arrangements don't come out perfectly fair and equal. Maybe
grandma is the preferred babysitter, but she's not available when
one twin needs to be looked after, so the less-favorite babysitter
is the only choice. As with all things twin (as well as with
different-age siblings), such inequities are inevitable. Learning
to cope with them will help your children adjust to life's realities.
The important thing is for each twin to experience being on his
own as he tries something new, meets new people, or has a new
adventure.

Separate playdates are another way to introduce the idea of
being apart from one's twin. Preschool age is a time when children want to get together to play with one special friend—to

spend time at another's house or to invite that person home and show him their room, their toys, their dog. For parents of twins, scheduling separate playdates requires twice the secretarial effort, but it is well worth it. The whole idea of providing a separate playdate for each child is so that your twins won't have to share a friend. Instead, they'll learn more about themselves and other kids, as well as the give and take of friendship, without the influence or interference of their same-age sibling.

In my experience as a twin and as a mother of twins, and in the experience of nearly all the parents in my groups, playdate threesomes that include twins simply don't work. Four-year-old brothers Leo and Brad are a case in point. Leo wanted to have his own playmate over, a boy he had met in preschool. The date was arranged, and the boy showed up with a box of his favorite building blocks to share with Leo. Leo and Brad's parents hadn't made arrangements for Brad to be somewhere else that day, so realizing that Leo needed time alone with his friend, they tried to get Brad to play alone in the den with his own toys. Brad was not a happy camper. He kept going into the bedroom where the two friends were playing, only to be brought back to the den by his dad. Crying that he wanted to play, too, he made his way back to the bedroom, screaming, crying, and kicking over the fort Leo and his friend had built. The parents finally asked Leo if he would be "nice enough" to include his brother in the playdate. By this time, though, the date was ruined. Brad felt hurt and left out and wouldn't stop crying, Leo was angry at his brother for interfering with his fun, and the friend was annoyed by Brad's loud and disruptive behavior.

Threesomes don't work. Even if Brad's hurt feelings hadn't resulted in a tantrum, the playdate wouldn't have been beneficial to Leo as long as his brother was expected to be part of it. Each twin needs to have friendships apart from his or her sibling, and Leo clearly made it known to his parents that he wanted the chance to have a solo playdate. Like many preschool-age kids, Leo and Brad each needed the opportunity to begin to define himself by choosing and learning to get along with a new friend on his own.

What can you do to prevent a Brad-like meltdown? When a playdate is scheduled for your house, either arrange for your other child to be out of the house—at a friend's, a neighbor's, a relative's, or with your spouse—or have him invite his own friend over. In the beginning, when your twins are getting used to the idea of separate playdates, you'll need to prepare for some resistance. The twin who won't be part of the playdate this time around (and who hasn't invited his own friend over this time) will complain, argue, and even cry that things are unfair. He will attempt to make you feel guilty with such protests as, "I'll be all alone with stupid Aunt Nancy, while he's having fun with a friend!!"

It will be hard for you to withstand such complaints at first, but try to hear your preschooler's resentment as developmental music to your ears. If Emma feels left out because her brother Christopher has a playdate, she will likely become more motivated to find and make her own friends. Wanting to enjoy the independent choices she sees her twin brother making will fuel Emma's innate drive to be her own person. Being challenged to strike out on her own as her same-age sibling is doing—in this case, by making her own friends—promotes healthy, age-appropriate growth. Eventually, both twins will gain the confidence to make friends of their own so that when one is having a playdate, the other won't be as jealous; each will know that their turn for a playdate of their own will be coming up soon.

As well adjusted to the idea of separate friends and play-dates as your twins become, there will still be those times when feelings are hurt, and parents are needed to soothe them. This happened in our family around the issue of birthday parties. Although Jonny and David had their own playdates and friends, there were a few times when one was invited to a friend's birthday party, and the other felt miserable about not being able to go. In fact, my husband and I reassured the parents of our boys' friends that inviting one and not both was fine—and appropriate. Why should Jonny be invited to David's friend's birthday party? Some parents felt compelled to invite both, and some parents would call us to discuss their discomfort about only including one. But we always felt that each boy should go to his own friend's party without being obligated to take his brother along.

Initially, hurt feelings and protests of injustice spewed forth from the excluded child. We empathized with his disappointment and told him that either my husband or I would be available on the day of the party to do something together. I don't mean that we would plan a special activity to rival the party, simply that he would spend some alone time with one of us. Smoothing over feelings of being left out is not always easy—or possible—but it is important to learn to cope with such feelings at a young age. While assuring the left-out twin that his turn to be invited to a party will come, you can also offer a sensitive, yet practical, "that's life" attitude. You might tell him something like, "Life isn't always fair or equal. And your life will always be different from your brother's, which is what makes each of you so special."

And speaking of birthday parties . . .

A Birthday Party of My Own

We started to have separate birthday parties for the boys when they turned three. It was uncomplicated in the sense that, since Jonny and David were in separate preschool groups, we invited each class to a separate party. Each boy was delighted with the idea of having his own party and choosing the theme for his invitations and decorations. Jonny was a Ninja Turtles fan when he was three, and David loved sports of all kinds, so their birthday cakes and our dining room were decorated accordingly. The only people who seemed uncomfortable with the idea of twins having separate birthday parties were some of the parents because, even though only one boy's name was on the invitation, they didn't know if they should get one present or two. When they asked, we explained that it was our wish that they do whatever they wanted, but that just one present for the birthday boy was appropriate.

I knew that separate birthday parties was the right way to go because I had experienced how it felt to have to share the limelight on the most special day of the year. Sharing a birthday party with my sister was all I ever knew when I was a child, and it wasn't until I had my three single children and began arranging birthday parties for them that I fully began to realize what I had missed. A birthday party, after all, is about celebrating a person's life; for a small child, it's about being the star for one day—having all the attention turned toward you and enjoying all your favorite things, from your favorite-flavor ice cream and cake to your most-loved cartoon character on the paper plates. When I was young, I never felt that my birthday was about me or the things I liked best. Jane's and my birthday parties were about the two of us as a matched set: one birthday cake, one party theme chosen by my mom, and usually two exactly-the-same presents from each of our guests. Always getting the same present meant that the first person to open the gift got to experience the surprise, and the other was robbed of that thrill. I'm sure our guests meant well, but for me it felt like an unfair disappointment. It was as if I were being penalized for being a twin because I couldn't enjoy the normal surprises and special feelings birthday girls (and boys) feel. When I became the mother of twins, I vowed to give my boys separate presents and separate birthday parties.

Of course, when twins receive different birthday presents, there is always the chance that each will wish for a particular present that the other one got. My husband and I handled this by telling our boys, "You each got what your guests chose for you. Your brother's gifts are his, and yours are yours. If you want to trade stuff, that's up to you—but only if you both want to."

Jonny and David grew up with the expectation that separate parties were the way our family did things. Our friends became accustomed to our separate-festivities routine and eventually felt comfortable with it. I know that Jonny and David really enjoyed their early birthday celebrations and appreciated having all the attention focused on just one boy on the day of the party. My husband and I were happy to provide them with the experience of celebrating their individuality on the occasion of their day of birth, shared though it may be.

As to scheduling two separate birthday parties, you might have one on Saturday and the second on Sunday. Or if you can't face two days in a row of party fever, you could have the second one on the following Saturday. There will likely be some complaining over who gets to have his party first. As hard as it is for young children to wait for something wonderful, you can assure the one whose party comes second this year that he will definitely be first next year.

Adjusting to Preschool on One's Own

Aside from traumatic events such as illness, divorce, death, and the birth of siblings, a child's first real test of coping with separation from his parents is his successful transition into preschool. For a few hours or more a day, the young child must cope by himself as he attempts to get along with other children and adapt to the rules and routines of authority figures other than his parents. Single children meet these challenges little by little, each child adjusting and developing according to his own timetable. For twins who have always played together and had little experience socializing on their own with other children, there is another important adjustment: separating from one's twin. Learning to get along in the new social environment of preschool, without the safety net of mom, dad, or one's constant partner, can be daunting for a two-, three-, or four-year-old. But your children will receive valuable benefits if you choose to take this separate, but developmentally advisable, route.

I firmly believe that enrolling each child in a separate preschool class ensures a very positive step forward toward self-assurance and social maturity. If you haven't yet provided your twins with separate activities and separate playmates, preschool is a wonderful opportunity to begin this process. But you can't do it abruptly. First, you'll have to allow them to attend class together, giving them time to adjust to the routine of preschool and separating from you for part of the day. This period of adjustment could last anywhere from a "semester" of three to six months to a full year. Then, once they've accommodated to the new environment and activities of preschool, they'll be ready to take the next step: being in a classroom without their twin.

If your children are already used to engaging in separate activities, separate preschool classes will strengthen their growing sense of self-discovery. The social benefits will be tremendous as each child experiences having other children, as well as adults, relate to him as separate and unique. When we made the decision to put Jonny and David in different classes in the same nursery school, a number of parents at the school wondered why we were separating our kids. The twin mystique was alive and well, and I was asked a number of times how each boy would adapt to being without his brother. I explained that my husband and I had always provided different activities for the boys, taking them to separate toddler groups and classes that each one enjoyed. David loved his junior karate class, while Jonny went for more creative, art-related activities. Enjoying separate preschool experiences was the continuation of a pattern we believed would help our boys develop into emotionally healthy individuals.

In my private practice and twin-parenting groups, I have seen what can happen when such separation doesn't occur. One set of three-year-old twin girls who had never been separated refused to talk to either the preschool teacher or the other children, using their twinship to cut themselves off from the class. The two had formed a singular unit as a way to avoid interacting with their new environment.

Another set of twins demonstrated a too-much-togetherness pattern that the preschool teacher was perceptive enough to detect.

The four-year-olds had established a routine whereby the sister told the brother what to do, and he obeyed. He rarely chose for himself what he wanted to play with or how he wanted to behave. Once they got to preschool, however, their teacher tried various strategies to get the sister to allow her brother to choose his own activities. When the little girl refused, the teacher advised the parents that the two needed to be placed into separate classes. The mom initially felt badly that the daughter was having such a hard time without her brother. I explained that the dominating twin is often the one who suffers more when a separation first occurs. I also advised her that we have to do our best to tolerate our children's distress when they're adjusting to something new so that they can work through it themselves and feel masterful. The preschool teacher had done these children a huge favor. The daughter needed to experience being away from her twin brother in order to learn to get along with children who won't be dominated. She needed to learn to be assertive, but not overbearing. And the son had the chance to develop friendships and interests on his own.

The initial situation with Anita's three-and-a-half-year-old sons was another example of what can happen when never-before-separated twins enter preschool in the same class. By the time Anita's twin boys were approaching their second birthday, it was becoming apparent that Nathan's development was lagging behind his brother Ben's. Nate screamed uncontrollably when noises bothered him. He didn't make eye contact or communicate with those around him and became lost in his world of toy animals and books. He was finally diagnosed as having Asperger's syndrome. Anita poured her energy into finding the best treatment strategies for Nathan. Meanwhile, she enrolled both Nathan and Ben in the same preschool class.

Anita told our group how Ben cared for Nathan at preschool. She described with maternal admiration, gratitude, and approval how Ben attempted to protect his brother from situations and children that he could not manage or master alone. While most of the mothers echoed Anita's admiring sentiments, I had a very different reaction. Although I appreciated Ben's nurturing behavior, I pointed out the potential negative repercussions of allowing him to be his brother's caretaker in class.

First of all, Nathan would struggle to learn how to get along on his own, despite the social challenges presented by his condition. With his brother there shielding him from other children and normal preschool activities, Nate was deriving few benefits from the group experience. And Ben's energies were so invested in taking care of his brother that he had little opportunity to socialize with the other children or to partake in activities he enjoyed.

After our discussions, Anita asked Ben how he felt about being in school with his brother. Ben was able to share with her that he felt mad about, and uncomfortable with, having to look out for Nathan all the time. He wanted to make his own friends and get involved in what the other kids were doing in class. Anita listened to Ben without judgment or resentment. She realized that it was not fair to put Ben in the position of having to take care of Nathan.

> *I guess it took me a little too long to admit I had made a mistake. Hearing the words from Ben himself shook me into the realization that he is entitled to be his own person. Taking care of Nathan is not his responsibility.*

Just because his brother has these problems doesn't
mean that Ben should suffer. I want him to feel free
to make friends and join in the activities that inter-
est him.

Anita decided to enroll the boys in different preschools. Ben was happy and relieved to be free from a burden that was not his to shoulder, and Nathan was able to attend a preschool that provided care and resources for children with special needs. Anita related that this was the best decision she had ever made. The brothers had a wonderful relationship and played well together at home, but they now had their own activities and social experiences. And Anita made the time to spend alone with each boy. "I have accepted that my boys are two separate children, and I'm trying to give them each what they need to grow and discover themselves," she told me.

When one twin is physically or mentally challenged, and the other isn't, it is important to remember that each child is a separate being with different needs and distinct life paths. The common parental desire to make things fair between twins is intensified when one child has special needs and, in fact, seems to need more of everything and everybody. Still, we should feel glad for the twin who has no physical or emotional problems and meets his developmental milestones while simultaneously feeling optimistic and hopeful for his brother, who has his own successes.

Anita talked about how hard it was when she arranged play-dates for Ben because it saddened her that children rarely wanted to play with Nathan, whose condition limited age-appropriate social behavior. But she hoped that he would begin to make friends at his new preschool. She coped with her boys' differences in a variety of ways. She made sure that she spent time alone with each child so that she could develop a close connection to each one. She answered Ben's questions about his brother's difficulties honestly and age-appropriately and encouraged him to share his ambivalent feelings regarding Nathan's behavior. She let Ben know that she wanted him to enjoy his school and his friends.

The honesty and openness between mother and each son, along with each brother's separate activities, will hopefully continue to foster a relationship between the two brothers that's not marked by obligation or embarrassment. And Anita found that talking to other mothers of special-needs children helped her enormously, especially as her boys' lives grew more divergent.

Waiting One's Turn

Has this ever happened to you? In an effort to be fair, you promise each twin that he'll have a turn—to take the dog for a walk with daddy, to have a friend over to play, or to have an alone-time ice-cream-cone date with mom. And then you end up feeling badly when one twin gets upset because it isn't his turn this time. So, you're tempted to give his turn to him then and there, thus depriving the other twin of his separate activity. In a word, don't. It's perfectly fine to be empathetic toward one child who's feeling left out; it's not appropriate for you to feel guilty and cave in. If you feel so sorry for the sad or angry preschooler who is not getting what he wants that you don't follow through with your plan to offer separate experiences, you unwittingly lend the twinship too much power over you. Your lack of parental backbone can contribute to your children's inability to respect you as the dependable authority figure. Young children, as well as older kids, need their parents to be consistent in adhering to rules. Otherwise, they feel lost and insecure because there is no one they can count on to control their impulsive behavior.

As much as you might think you're doing the right thing by minimizing the competitive struggles between your twins and giving in to their demand for "fairness," you'll be seriously undermining your parental control and your children's sense of security. Caving in to a preschooler's demands is common among parents of singletons as well, but the situation is doubly troublesome with twins because you'll have to endure the whining and nagging of two children who know they can get the best of you if they simply complain long enough.

There is a healthier way to deal with the disappointed twin who feels left out when he has to wait his turn, and it's similar to the method that nursery school teachers employ. Compassionately assure your child that if he waits—until later in the day or tomorrow, for instance—and is respectful of his brother's turn, he will have his own time to enjoy what he wants without having to share the time with his brother. You might even remind him, "When it's your turn to go for ice cream with me, your brother will have to wait."

This is the age of learning to tolerate frustration and control one's disappointment, and it's not an easy lesson, which is why teaching impulse control, as well as modeling appropriate social behavior, is an important parental responsibility. When a young child learns that he can't have exactly what he wants at precisely the moment he wants it—in this case, at the same time his twin brother is receiving it—he'll be well on his way toward becoming a big kid.

Why Is Alone Time
So Important Now?

Encouraging each child to think of herself as a separate person is especially crucial during the preschool years. That's because this phase of development involves furthering a child's sense of herself and how she is distinct from others. Therefore, making an effort to establish your unique connection with each twin through alone time is particularly critical now. Spending time with your preschooler involves more conversation than during babyhood, and you'll learn about her not only through what she talks about but how she navigates the world around her as the two of you explore your environment and each other. Being alone with you gives each child the chance to see herself reflected in your eyes, in your reactions to what she's doing and saying. It may not seem that this is an important aspect of her emotional growth, but it is. You are helping her find out who she is even when the two of you are merely folding laundry together, drinking hot chocolate at your local café, or throwing a ball back and forth at the park.

When parents assume that their twins are happy simply being with each other and don't need one-on-one time with mom or dad, the result can be a reneging on the parental role and subsequent feelings of abandonment in each child. The twins may then gradually shut their parents out and attempt to meet each other's needs. Rather than the parent's having the all-important individual connection with each child, the twinship becomes the core relationship. Creating a close threesome—parent and two children—likewise cannot substitute for the one-on-one relationship between one parent and one child. Parents must be more influential in the lives of each twin than the other twin. If this is not established early on, emotional and social problems can arise.

Alone time with each child is also particularly important at this time because it can contribute to your child's language development. Research suggests that some twins develop language skills more slowly because they often spend less time alone with their parents and fewer words are spoken to each child. Young children need their parents to focus repetitively on individual words in order to reinforce their meaning and pronunciation. Thus, it's beneficial if you or your partner can be alone with each child for at least a little while. What I'm suggesting doesn't involve formalized word games or computer programs; simply talking with each child one-on-one is time well spent.

Remind Yourself Not to Compare

There are so many developmental milestones to be reached during the preschool years that parents are understandably concerned about their children's arriving at each of them "on time." But there is such a wide range of time within which it is considered "normal" for a child to learn to talk, use the potty, recognize letters and numbers, and socialize with peers that it doesn't make sense for parents to drive themselves crazy worrying that their children will never "get it." One concerned mom told me that one of her three-year-old twins barely spoke more than a few sentences, while the other already used sophisticated language. I assured her that twins can develop at very different rates, just like unrelated children of the same age. Oh, and by the way, I mentioned, Albert Einstein didn't learn to talk until he was four.

Whether or not either of your twins becomes a little Einstein, it's important to remember that they will proceed along different timetables as they strive to master their preschool skills. As your children mature, you will always be tempted to compare their strengths and struggles, but it's best to see their developmental differences as a blessing because they help you acknowledge that each twin is unique. Two different children, whether they're fraternal or identical twins, are developing within their own time frames. How you respond to each child's individual differences can affect how they feel about themselves.

As preschool-age twins struggle to become unique individuals, we need to celebrate their diversity rather than be worried or uncomfortable when one takes longer than the other to learn the alphabet or one runs like a marathoner while the other takes his own sweet time. Just because they're twins doesn't mean they're traveling to the beat of the same drum.

Parents-of-Twins Journal: The Preschool Years

WRITE DOWN YOUR THOUGHTS

- If one of your twins tends to be the caretaker of the other, how does this make you feel?
- How has each child shown you that he may want his own possessions, his own space, or his own private time, separate from his same-age sibling?
- What behaviors do your twins exhibit that lead you to believe they might be experiencing too much togetherness?

- How has each child adjusted to preschool? What effect do you think being in the same class or separate classes has had?
- What have you learned about each child during your alone time with each one?

Tips for Parents of Preschool-Age Twins

- If one child is having a hard time making her own choices and tends to mimic her sister in choosing what to play with or what to wear, help her out by suggesting something like, "You are different from your sister, and you can make different choices. Why don't you choose the toy that you like the best."
- If you want to insure that each child has the chance to develop his own friendships, make sure that when you arrange a playdate in your home, either the other twin is out of the house or has his own friend over to play with.
- Talk to the administrator, teachers, or both at your children's preschool and make sure that they understand your philosophy about nurturing individuality in your twins. Let them know that you want to encourage each child to pursue her or his own friendships and interests.
- Don't be shy about explaining your twin philosophy to other parents whose children play with your kids. Let them know, for example, that they need only invite the child who is their child's friend on a playdate or to a birthday party.

- It's a myth that twins don't fight; they do, and sometimes more aggressively, because they are together so much of the time and competing for their share of the parent's time, attention, praise, and recognition. And even preschoolers get frustrated at not having their own space and time to themselves. Unless they're physically hurting each other, allow your twins to have squabbles and help them learn how to resolve conflicts through negotiation and problem solving. Alone time with each twin can help you understand what may be causing too many fights.

· six ·

ELEMENTARY SCHOOL KIDS

When Jenna came home with her Science Achievement Award, I told her I was proud of her and that I'd buy a nice frame for the certificate, which she could hang in her room. But I also told her not to talk about the award in front of her twin brother. Shane had been struggling in both math and science and would be lucky to get Cs. I didn't want Jenna's success to make Shane feel like a failure. Only later did I realize that I had asked Jenna to hide her achievement to protect her brother, who was having difficulties in his science class.

—JANET, MOTHER OF EIGHT-YEAR-OLD TWINS

The elementary school years lay the foundation for a child's academic life, as well as usher in a time of growing independence and major social strides. As your children pursue a prescribed school curriculum, they will also get involved in outside interests such as soccer, piano, chess, and karate. Their lives will no longer revolve solely around you and your family; school will become like a second home. Their studies, friendships, and after-school activities will begin to teach them about the world and how they might fit into it. For twins, elementary school presents additional challenges and opportunities. Competition with one's same-age sibling can seem intense and unavoidable. Teachers, school officials, and classmates may unintentionally undermine each child's sense of individuality by focusing on the twin mystique rather than what each boy or girl is really about. At the same time, a school environment offers each twin the chance to develop intellectually, follow her own individual interests, and make her own friends.

In this chapter, we'll explore the frustration and shame that can accompany the inevitable academic and social differences between twins and what you can do to help each child deal with them. Hiding one twin's achievements to prevent the other from feeling badly, as Jenna's mom suggested, is not a healthy strategy. Letting each child know that she will always have different strengths than her brother, however, prepares her for a lifetime of differences. We'll also talk about what it feels like to get attention just for being a twin and how this can make it difficult for your children to initiate authentic friendships. And I'll give you advice on how to help your twins handle being in separate classrooms or going away to separate summer camps.

First, let's take a look at current school policies concerning the educational placement of twins and why some parents are attempting to change the rules.

Twins in Separate Classrooms: For and Against

After psychological research in the 1970s and 1980s began focusing on the serious problems that can occur when twins are not separated, educational authorities concluded that, in order to help strengthen twins' sense of individuality, twins should have separate classroom experiences. Consequently, school boards began implementing regulations stipulating that twins be placed in separate classrooms beginning in kindergarten. It was believed that each child needs to have separate experiences from her twin in order to develop according to her own unique academic and social potential, as I have espoused throughout this book. School officials felt that, too often, having twins in the same classroom created an unhealthy interdependence that inhibited each child from learning at her own pace, pursuing her own interests, and making her own friends.

Many parents of twins, however, oppose the separate-classroom policy. They feel that parents, not school officials, ought to be the ones to make decisions about whether or not to place their twins in the same classroom. Some parents argue that it can be traumatic and detrimental for their twin children to be separated, and there are growing grassroots parental movements to change school placement policies concerning twins.

Where do I stand on the controversy? I obviously believe in separate experiences for twins, but as I mentioned in the last chapter, I don't think it is advisable to separate young twin children abruptly. If your children have been in separate preschool classes, or if they are well adjusted to separate activities prior to kindergarten, then being placed in separate classes will be a smooth transition for them. If they haven't yet had the experience of separating from their twin, then it's probably best to have them placed in the same classroom for a year while they adjust to kindergarten. If your school or school district has a separate-classroom policy regarding twins, it may be possible to negotiate with the appropriate authorities to allow your children to be placed together initially. Many parents have successfully done so. The National Organization of Mothers of Twins Club (NOMOTC) has a brochure entitled "Guidelines for the Education of Multiple Birth Children" that can serve as a template for negotiating with school authorities. You might also be interested in finding out more about how the state legislatures in Minnesota and Texas have passed laws stipulating the parents' right to choose when it is appropriate for their twins to be placed in separate classrooms.

While it is certainly important to have a say in school policies affecting your twins, your overall objective will be to make sure that each child can enjoy his own unique school experience. At age five, many children are capable of handling themselves on their own in a more demanding environment than preschool, and twins should feel no less empowered to succeed at this task.

When your children are in separate kindergarten classes, it will be normal for them to compare notes: "In my class, the teacher does it this way." "Oh, no, in my class we do this." There may even be quarrels over whose class is better. As parents, we can nonchalantly reaffirm that we all have different experiences, and that's fine. The important thing is that each child feels comfortable learning and making friends on her own without the emotional support of her same-age sibling.

Often, well-meaning teachers, relatives, and parents get so caught up in the fear that twins won't be able to make it on their own, or in the attempt to make things fair between them, that they lose sight of what each twin really needs: her own classroom experience and a teacher and classmates who perceive her as an individual, rather than as one-half of a couple.

One Loves His Independence, the Other Doesn't: A Kindergarten Story

Five-year-old twins Carlos and Jesse reacted to their separate kindergarten classroom experiences in starkly different ways. Carlos raced into his dad's arms at the end of the first day of school, excited to tell him about the painting he had made, the puzzle he had put together, and the new friend who sat next to him at lunch. Jesse appeared forlorn and upset, and when his father asked him how his first day went, he replied, "Horrible!" As the weeks went by, Carlos continued to flourish, while Jesse remained hesitant and gloomy.

Kindergarten was the first chance either boy had had to be apart from the other. In preschool, Jesse had been clingy around his brother, placing Carlos in the unwanted role of caretaker. Their parents had not arranged for separate activities for either boy prior to kindergarten, with the exception of occasional play-dates that Carlos was invited to. (No one had ever asked Jesse on a playdate because he only seemed interested in playing with his brother.) Now that the brothers were forced to be in separate classrooms, Carlos was enjoying his freedom from his brother, while Jesse was still trying to cling to him. At recess, he would seek out Carlos and attempt to hone in on his playground games with his new friends. Carlos would tell him, "Leave me alone," but Jesse persisted—and told his parents, "Carlos is always mean to me and won't let me play with him. It's not fair!" The boys' father took Carlos aside and told him he should try to be nicer to Jesse, that he wasn't acting like the loving brother he had always been. "You used to be best friends. What happened?"

What had happened was not only a positive turn of events but also a normal developmental milestone. Carlos was staking out his own social territory and making the most of his new-found independence. Jesse was miserable as he began the process of learning to manage without the emotional support of his brother, but he, too, was going through the necessary steps toward self-reliance. In my conversations with Jesse and Carlos's parents, I explained that Carlos had been unfairly saddled with the job of coparenting his twin brother. This is not the role a child ought to take on. Mom and dad wanted Jesse to be as independent and as well adjusted to kindergarten as Carlos was, but they had to give Carlos permission to give up his caretaker role, which he was relinquishing on his own quite nicely. Jesse had the potential to get along socially without his brother's assistance; his parents just needed to believe in his ability to do so and to communicate that belief to him. As long as they held onto the counterproductive notion that twins should be best friends and each other's caretakers, they were undermining each child's healthy strides toward self-determination.

I encouraged Jesse and Carlos's parents to have Jesse invite a friend from his class over for a playdate. And when Carlos expressed the desire to have his own room, I helped the parents understand that as a healthy sign, rather than a severing of the boys' relationship. It took Jesse a lot longer to adjust to the kindergarten separation from his brother than it had taken Carlos, who made the adjustment on day one. With the bumpy road of kindergarten behind him, however, Jesse found that being in a first-grade classroom without his twin brother was much easier.

The Perils of Twin Dependency

Even when twins are placed in separate classrooms, their dependency on each other can continue at an unhealthy level. The longer this dependency is maintained, the more difficult it will be for one of them, or for both, to adjust once they are called upon to separate from each other. Most of us are familiar with the term "separation anxiety" as it applies to preschool-age children who are insecure and fearful when they must adjust to being without mom or dad for periods of time. Twins who never learn to separate from each other may also face separation anxiety when they are finally parted. I refer to this as "twin separation anxiety." The story of Rachel and Kristen sheds light on what can happen when twins remain emotionally dependent on each other throughout elementary school, then one takes a different path, leaving the other to cope with her sister's absence.

Rachel and Kristen attended the same elementary school but, due to school policies, were always placed in separate classes. Rachel was the dominant sister, and her identity was essentially defined by being Kristen's caretaker. On the playground, at lunch time, and before and after school, she told Kristen what to do; asked her for a rundown on what had happened in her class that day; made sure other kids treated Kristen in a manner that she, Rachel, determined to be fair; and generally bossed Kristen around.

Kristen was known as a people person. Other children were drawn to her outgoing personality and fun-loving ways. While Rachel was a perfectionist who habitually got good grades, Kristen was less academic but more creative. She had a wonderful imagination, although some might say she lived in a dream world. Rachel was disciplined and hardworking, whereas Kristen didn't like to settle down long enough to do her homework and didn't seem interested in conforming to the rules. After Kristen and Rachel's mom noticed that Kristen's grades had declined and that she was struggling with her work, the teacher informed her that Kristen had a slight learning disability. It was suggested that she transfer to a smaller school where she could get more individualized attention.

So, in the fourth grade, Kristen transferred to another school. Her mother reported that Kristen was the happiest she had ever been. "She loves her class and her teacher, and she's having a wonderful time meeting new kids," she told me. Rachel, however, had great difficulty adjusting. She suffered from severe separation anxiety and appeared to lose self-confidence. Her struggle lasted several months, during which time she demonstrated intense fear of being separated from her mother, something that preschoolers go through but that Rachel had not experienced due to her close attachment to her twin sister.

Rachel had been so coupled with her twin sister that when their relationship was altered by Kristen's departure to another school and Rachel's domineering role no longer defined who she was, Rachel fell apart. She no longer felt secure within herself and dreaded going to school in the morning, pleading with her mother by saying, "I'll miss you too much, Mommy!" As one would do for a preschooler or kindergartener, Rachel's mother pasted a picture of herself into Rachel's lunchbox, along with notes saying, "I love you, Rachel. You're going to be fine today." She also told Rachel she could call her at recess and at lunch.

The pictures and phone calls weren't enough to quell Rachel's insecurity. She continued to be anxious and to cling to her mother like a much younger child would do. She even got upset when her parents went out at night, telling her mother she wanted her to be with her, not her dad. "Why do you always have to go out with him instead of being with me?" she would cry. Rachel's clinging behavior toward her mother was a desperate attempt to be part of another couple. She wanted to replace her sister with her mother in order to stave off the feeling of having lost her place in the world, of not belonging.

Rachel no longer wanted to ride with the other carpool parents because she felt unsafe, wanting her mother to drive her to school instead, and she refused to go out to dinner with her parents' friends who were visiting from out of town, saying she was scared to be with them, even though she had known the couple for years. She cried and screamed when her parents were about to head out for "back-to-school" night at her school, protesting that she didn't want them to leave her. Things had gotten so bad that Rachel's mom was considering transferring her to Kristen's school.

What were the specific issues underlying Rachel's severe separation anxiety? She was filled with rage at her sister and her mother for leaving her on her own at the old school. Her overwhelming fear stemmed from feeling out of control. Without Kristen, whom she had depended on her whole life to help her transition into new situations, Rachel now had to rely on her own inner resources to face the social forces of elementary school. Prior to Kristen's transferring to the new school, the twinship had served as a barrier against those forces, a united front that masked Rachel's tenuous sense of self. While it had always seemed that she was the stronger of the two because she was "the bossy one," in fact Rachel needed Kristen more than Kristen needed her. Kristen was doing just fine in her new school; she had no difficulty adjusting to her new academic and social environment. But Rachel needed help to make it through this difficult period of adjustment. She had to learn to separate emotionally not only from her sister but from her mother as well.

I suggested that Rachel's mom continue to express confidence in Rachel's ability to make new friendships and feel stronger at school. She could encourage Rachel to try making friends through her hobbies—by joining the drama club at school, for instance. If mom spent more alone time with Rachel (as well as with Kristen), it would create a stronger bond between them, thereby allowing Rachel to feel more secure. Paradoxically, the focused one-on-one time together would encourage Rachel's independence by strengthening her awareness of herself as a unique individual, thus her belief in herself. I also advised that it would be a good idea for Rachel and Kristen to have separate bedrooms, given that the family had an extra room they were only occasionally using as a guest room. Still taken with the notion that the girls should be best friends and believing that separate bedrooms would interfere with their relationship, Rachel and Kristen's parents were skeptical about this suggestion.

Six months later, I learned that Rachel was doing much better. She had made new friends at school, had developed a close relationship with a girl in her drama group, and had just tried out for a role in a play. Rachel and Kristen's mom was relieved that she hadn't given in to Rachel's anxiety by transferring her to Kristen's school. She told me that some of her friends who were parents of twins were aghast that she had placed her daughters in separate schools. They told her that they would never consider separating their twins, especially if one showed signs of being unhappy. I told her that she was not alone in fielding critical reactions from those who were still enthralled and intimidated by the twin mystique. The proof of her wise decision was clear to see: both Rachel and Kristen were thriving.

I Want to Be Liked for Me

You might not think that a child would protest, "Everyone likes me too much!" Being liked for the wrong reasons, however, can feel uncomfortable, even when you're not old enough to articulate this. Having the kids at school like you because you're half of a cute pair of twins can make you feel that you're getting away with something you don't deserve, that you haven't earned the right to your notoriety or to someone's friendship. Worse, you sense that others don't see who you really are. In fact, what they seem to value is merely the circumstances of your birth. You and your twin happened to be born on the same day: so what? Even if your parents have taught you from an early age to be your own person and to develop your own interests apart from your same-age sister or brother, when others lavish attention on you simply for being a twin, you're not sure how to respond.

If you enjoy an honest, open relationship with your children so that they feel free to talk with you about their concerns, you can discuss this issue with them and perhaps offer some suggestions. Here's an example of how a conversation about being liked too much for being a twin might go between you and your nine-year-old:

YOUR CHILD: The kids at school are so stupid!
YOU: Why do you say that?
YOUR CHILD: They think I'm really cool because I'm a twin.
YOU: And do you think you're cool?
YOUR CHILD: I don't know. I'm a good soccer player . . . and I'm funny. But it has nothing to do with being a twin.
YOU: Maybe you could tell the kids at school that.

When I was growing up, everyone was curious about the blonde identical twins Jane and Joan. We were special and adorable, and few people could tell us apart. We dressed alike, had similar hairstyles, and had matching alliterative names. Throughout elementary school, the other kids sought us out and afforded Jane and me ongoing celebrity status. But I can also remember how intrusive and meaningless it sometimes felt getting so much attention just because I happened to look like someone else. Jane and I relished the idea of being noticed, but had we been able to put words to our feelings, I think we each would have said that we wished we could be acknowledged for things about us that had nothing to do with being a twin—like the hypothetical child in the above conversation. What he finds "cool" about himself is that he's a good soccer player and he's funny. Being thought of as "cool" just for being a twin seems completely pointless.

A child's developing sense of self is not nourished simply by being noticed; rather, it is fed by being seen for who he really is and who he is trying to become. One's athletic strengths, sense of humor, ability to be a trusted friend: these are things an elementary school–aged child might value in himself and would hope others would recognize in him as well. Being popular because he has a look-alike or fraternal twin and having a fuss made over his twinness can diminish a child's sense of self. Being noticed and being known are not synonymous.

If one of your twins comes to you with this concern, let him know, first of all, that it's okay to have ambivalent feelings about being a twin. It's okay to enjoy lots of things about being a twin and, at the same time, not to enjoy being liked just because you're a twin. Many twins are never given the opportunity to articulate the things that bother them about having a twin brother or sister. Give your child the chance to voice his negative feelings—in this case, about being treated as an oddity, albeit a "cool" one. You may have to initiate this conversation yourself; if you wait for your child to bring up the subject on his own, it may not happen.

A number of parents of twins have told me that one child will invite a friend over only to be asked, "Is your twin going to be there?" It's clear to the disappointed twin that the main reason the kid wants to play with him is to be around "the twins." Again, being liked for something that has nothing to do with who you really are doesn't make a child feel very good. So, encourage each twin to have separate playdates, and make sure neither child has to share his friend with his sibling. Getting close to a friend on a one-to-one basis will allow each child to experience being known and liked as himself.

Disciplining One and Not the Other

There are often unintended consequences when parents attempt to be "fair and equal" with their twins. Although the impulse to treat each child the same stems from the desire to show that you love each one equally, each child actually needs you to demonstrate that you understand who she is as an individual. One of the ways we do this is by paying attention to each child's individual behavior and responding to it accordingly. When that behavior isn't in line with your family's rules, the child needs to be given consequences that will teach her to do better next time. And if her twin doesn't have to suffer the same consequences? Get ready to offer up the recurring lesson that "you and your sister/brother are not the same person," which, unfortunately, Carol failed to impart.

Carol's six-year-old daughters, Zoe and Kate, seemed to be constantly embroiled in a fight. The prevalent dynamic was that when Kate wasn't getting her own way, she would call Zoe names and physically push her around. Zoe, who was less aggressive than her sister, would nonetheless retaliate with her own not-so-diplomatic accusations. The fights would escalate into high-pitched screaming matches, at which point Carol would intervene. Carol tried various strategies to put an end to the fighting but was left feeling angry at, and powerless over, her inability to control the situation. She finally decided to try a positive-reinforcement approach, which involved awarding each girl points for good behavior. Once either girl earned enough points, she would be entitled to a coveted Hello Kitty tote bag. Zoe had no difficulty accumulating the required number of points since she tended to be more easygoing and less antagonistic than her sister. Kate wanted a Hello Kitty bag every bit as much as Zoe, but even with such a prized incentive, she was not always able to censor her name-calling and yelling outbursts. She was five points away from earning the plush pink bag when Zoe reached her goal.

Unfortunately, Carol was so uncomfortable with the fact that Zoe would get the Hello Kitty bag and Kate wouldn't, she actually cheated on Kate's behalf. This well-meaning mom, who couldn't tolerate any disparity between her twins, surreptitiously added points to Kate's good-behavior chart so that it appeared she had earned the bag, just as Zoe had. Since Kate knew she hadn't actually earned the tote bag, what lessons did this six-year-old come away with? Perhaps one or more of the following:

Elementary School Kids / 151

- I don't ever have to try very hard because Mommy will always do it for me.
- It doesn't matter if I can't control my temper; I'll be rewarded anyway.
- I will always be able to have exactly what my twin sister gets.

And what about Zoe? She knew that her sister had not behaved well enough to earn the Hello Kitty bag. What lessons was she left with? Most likely, one or more of these:

- Mommy can't protect me from Kate's bad behavior.
- Since I can't trust Mommy to tell the truth and stand up for what's right, I'll have to go along with whatever Kate wants.
- It doesn't pay to be truthful.
- Kate and I will always be treated the same, no matter what.

Are these really the lessons we want to teach our children? Carol had only intended to cut Kate a little slack; after all, her behavior had improved slightly, hadn't it? Still, Carol had to admit that her underlying motive for "fixing" the good-behavior chart was her own need to make things equal between her daughters. Her fear that twins can't possibly tolerate being treated differently—thus her inability to discipline Kate—led Carol to send her children some harmful messages.

- Kate, not Mommy, is in control.
- Mommy can't be trusted to give us consequences that are fair.

Ironically, in an attempt to be fair and equal with her twins, Carol was not only unfair but also untruthful, which brings us to the general question of disciplining twins. If we can think of our twin children as we would nontwin siblings, disciplining or rewarding only the deserving one makes good sense. Rather than coming away with the confusing and unsettling messages that Kate and Zoe received, your children will learn that mom or dad can accurately assess a child's individual behavior and will consistently discipline or reward that child accordingly. It does not make good parenting sense, as Carol eventually learned, to treat both children the same just because they're twins.

What Are They Really Fighting About?

When we think of sibling rivalry between singletons, we tend to approach it as an inevitable occurrence—annoying for parents to deal with, perhaps, but nothing to panic over. We assume that nontwin siblings will go through periods of not getting along, fighting over every little thing, even being downright nasty to each other, and we chalk this up to a typical form of competitiveness that has to do with children defining who they are by opposing the peer they're closest to. We also understand that sisters and brothers vie for love and attention from their parents and that they try to impress mom or dad with their accomplishments in the hope that it will cast them in a brighter light than their siblings. Parents hope that a good relationship between brothers and sisters will develop eventually, but they're prepared for the expected friction bearing a label they're well familiar with: sibling rivalry. While some parents are overwhelmed by the degree of hostility that can erupt among siblings, they are nonetheless aware that it's all part of a normal phase of their children's development.

Given the more intense rivalry for their parents' attention, as well as the challenges twins face in defining themselves as separate from their twin, we should expect even greater sibling rivalry between them. Thanks to the twin mystique, however, when same-age brothers and sisters fight, parents worry that something must be terribly wrong. After all, aren't twins supposed to be best friends with an unbreakable bond that guards against any potential animosity? Why would any child want to come to blows or even exchange harsh words with the one person in the world who best understands him and to whom he feels most closely connected?

Placing such expectations on your twin children is not only unrealistic, but it can also be harmful to their healthy emotional development. Twins have an even greater need than singletons to compete for their parents' love and to define themselves as separate from their same-age sibling. They should be given the same permission to squabble with their sister or brother without its being thought of as a major catastrophe. In fact, I'm more worried when parents tell me that their twins don't fight because it often means that neither child has permission to voice his feelings. Neither feels safe enough to go against the wishes of the other for fear that the twinship will somehow be put at risk. But children should have a sense of themselves as individuals, not as members of a couple that needs to be propped up at all costs.

With that said, what are the normal parameters of sibling rivalry between twins? Here are some typical rival behaviors that you can expect from your school-age twins:

- accusing parents of showing preference for one twin over the other
- fighting over who gets more of . . . whatever
- one twin's blaming the other for using or ruining his or her belongings
- insisting that one twin "copies" the other . . . whatever
- competition for the parents' attention and approval
- demands for "proof" that the parent loves one twin as much as, or more than, the other

Are there instances when sibling rivalry between twins crosses the line into overly aggressive, troubling behavior? The story of Martin and Jack serves as a cautionary tale of what can happen when twins are so frustrated at not being seen by their parents as separate individuals that their anger builds to a dangerous level.

Angela came to our twin-parenting group appearing to be only moderately alarmed by what was going on between her nine-year-old sons. She told us that they were having physical fights, which often ended up with one being cut, bruised, punched, or whacked by the other. It seemed to me that the impulsive aggressive behavior she described was quite out of control, yet Angela appeared oblivious to the severity of the situation.

She described her son Martin as the "good twin," who closely resembled his father in temperament and personality. He did very well in school and seemed smarter than his twin brother, Jack, she said. Martin was also more successful at making friends, but because Jack was so "over the top," Martin's friends didn't want to have anything to do with Jack. When it came to describing Jack, Angela did so entirely in negative terms. He was immature, misbehaved in school, and was never able to keep up with Martin's academic performance. Jack was often left at home with a babysitter during family outings because his behavior was disruptive and inappropriate.

After Angela had finished, another member of the group who knew Jack and Martin because they'd been at her house to play with her children offered her description of Jack.

> It's true Jack can be argumentative and aggressive, but I've noticed that he's also very creative. When he's at our house, I sometimes give him art supplies and set him up at the dining room table, and he really gets into it. I think he enjoys being able to be alone and not have to relate to the others. I can tell he's relieved that I've figured out what he really wants and that I let him know that's okay. Maybe he just needs to be off on his own sometimes. It definitely calms him down.

It was interesting to watch Angela as she listened to another person's description of Jack. It was as if she had never considered that her son might have another side to him. In her mind, Jack was defined by all the ways in which he didn't match up to his "smarter," more mature, better-behaved brother.

Other group members began to discuss the importance of treating twins as separate beings. One strategy they talked about was creating opportunities for the expression of each child's individual interests. Angela seemed startled by this new perspective but interested in what the others had to say. I also explained that the physical aggression between her boys could very likely be a reflection of their frustration at not being recognized as separate people with separate needs.

It seemed to me that Jack's behavior was a reaction to his parents' disappointment over their twin sons' being so unalike. Angela and her husband looked upon Jack's personality as a refusal to conform to the family's social and academic expectations. I gently explained to Angela that children show us through their behavior what is troubling them. Jack's acting out was a clue to understanding his unhappiness about a situation in which he felt victimized and helpless. He couldn't seem to fit in with Martin's friends or the kinds of things Martin liked to do, and his parents didn't understand his predicament. Angela said she would consider the feedback we had given her and attempt to provide separate experiences for Jack that were more geared toward his interests and personality. Unfortunately, she didn't quite follow through with her plan; she continued to perceive Jack and Martin as a biological couple who shouldn't be separated.

A few months later, Angela shared a heart-wrenching incident. She had sent Jack to a birthday party that only Martin had been invited to. Angela had been annoyed that the birthday boy had excluded Jack, so she sent him anyway. About an hour after she dropped both boys off at the party, she received a phone call from the birthday boy's mother demanding that Angela come and take Jack home. The hostess frantically informed Angela that Jack had destroyed the birthday cake, physically assaulted some of the children, and smeared the furniture with ice cream and frosting.

When Angela arrived at the party, she found Jack sobbing uncontrollably on the couch. At that moment, the prophetic words of our group members resonated within her. She had failed to attend to Jack's needs by stubbornly insisting he follow in Martin's footsteps—and in this case, insisting he attend a party to which he hadn't been invited. Angela lovingly took Jack home and apologized for making the wrong decision in sending him to the party. She realized that she had been treating Jack in accordance with her own desire for him to match up to Martin, rather than appreciating who Jack really was and what he needed.

Within six months or so, the rivalry between Jack and Martin abated somewhat, and Jack's behavior improved. Angela allowed Jack to make more of his own decisions about whom he wanted to socialize with and which after-school activities he wanted to participate in. She and her husband planned to have separate bedrooms for the boys in the new home they were building. There was even talk of placing them in separate schools. Meanwhile, Jack had gone to see a therapist for a few sessions, but Angela decided he didn't need to go back because the fights with his brother had subsided, and Jack seemed more relaxed. She and her husband had made practical changes that had resulted in some positive results, but they were still uncomfortable discussing emotional issues with either Jack or Martin.

I attempted to explain to Angela that the relationship between Jack and the therapist would be valuable and healing for Jack since his father was often unavailable. It was not enough that Jack's behavior had improved; his feelings needed to be articulated and understood by a trusted adult. Feeling somewhat stigmatized by their son's need to see a therapist, Angela and her husband decided to take a wait-and-see stance.

Jack and Martin's story dramatically points to the need for parents to accept their children's differences. Sibling rivalry and fighting between twins is normal; lashing out the way Jack did is not. As parents, we need to understand that a child's aggressive behavior is a desperate attempt to communicate that something is wrong. It is our responsibility to find out what that is and address it.

Academic Differences

What do you do when one twin brings home a report card with all As, the other brings home one with mostly Cs, and both are putting in an equal amount of effort? Like Janet, who worried that her daughter's science award would make her C-average son feel like a failure, as parents of twins we can't help but feel badly for the child who is having a tougher time in school than his same-age sibling. But perhaps we need to explore what's behind our worries and bad feelings.

As much as we believe in treating twins as individuals and avoiding the temptation to compare, we may not always be able to practice what we preach. Understandably, parents of twins are even more inclined than parents of singleton siblings to judge one child's achievements against the other's. This is due in large part to the twin mystique asserting that twins are uncannily alike in countless ways. So, how can one twin not get As when the other does? Even when we don't mean to, and even if we don't voice our "he does, so why don't you?" twin logic, we're too often guilty of comparing our twins. Our kids can sense when we're comparing them, and this makes them compare themselves to their twin as well.

If, on the other hand, we have made it clear to each child that he is on his own individual path and that his successes and challenges will be different from his twin's, both children will be more accepting of their differences. If Janet assured Shane all along that putting forth his best effort was what was most important, if she had refrained from comparing his grades to his sister Jenna's, and if she had made sure to acknowledge Shane's successes in other areas of his life, chances are Shane would be able to handle his sister's limelight moments. He would know there would be moments for him as well, maybe not having to do with school work but in other parts of his life. Maybe he was learning to play an instrument or was a terrific catcher on his Little League team. Perhaps he was a people person, and among his strengths was the ability to be a school leader or a wonderful friend. Maybe he made other people laugh or was particularly helpful with an elderly relative or a younger sibling. Children develop a vast range of positive attributes over the course of childhood, and many of these aren't reflected on a report card. After all, isn't it possible that a person's success in life has to do with more than how well he or she does in school?

We all want our children to shine academically, and as if our own aspirations for them weren't enough, today's culture seems to be pushing parents ever harder to assure that their kids get every possible academic advantage—beginning with educational tools for one-year-olds! We can certainly make sure that our children get the extra help they need when they're having a hard time in a particular subject. Tutors are often available through the school, and if not, we can hire one. If, however, one of our twins is doing her best and still not performing as well as we might hope, we may just have to face the reality that not everyone gets As. And that's okay.

Cheering for Two Teams, Packing for Two Camps

Throughout their elementary school years, we continued our commitment to providing separate experiences for Jonny and David, which included separate after-school sports teams. Although this created scheduling headaches and calendar overload, it gave each boy the opportunity to enjoy team camaraderie without the interference or influence of his brother. And our whole family enjoyed it when Jonny's and David's Little League or soccer teams played against each other. Of course, there were those in the stands who gave us strange looks when they heard us cheering for both teams.

Some parents seemed surprised by Robert's and my ability to enjoy the fact that our sons were competing against one another. "Isn't it hard," they would ask, "to watch your twins playing for opposing sides?" We felt these moms and dads were taking the competition thing way too seriously, first of all. And secondly, they failed to understand that the boys' athletic competitiveness was a healthy sign. Each kid appreciated being able to show the other and the rest of the family that he had individual strengths, both on the playing field and in the dugout.

When I was in elementary school, I always had the sense that a healthy rivalry between my twin sister and me was unacceptable. If one of us was involved in an activity, the other had to be right there alongside her. We were a permanent team of two. I would have loved to have quit that "team" in order to pursue my own interests, but instead I had to deny my negative feelings about our forced togetherness. Watching my sons on separate teams served as a metaphor for the natural competition between them, which made each boy feel that he was putting forth his own best effort.

In addition to being on separate sports teams and in separate classrooms, Jonny and David had very different elementary school experiences. Jonny enjoyed more artistic pursuits, while David enjoyed sports, sports, and more sports. David struggled academically, but he was more outgoing than Jonny and made friends easily. Jonny was shy and reticent about extending himself to others. He made a good friend the first day of kindergarten and remained close to that boy for many years. David had a wider circle of friends and enjoyed the constant flow of new social contacts.

In spite of all the separations that we had orchestrated for Jonny and David, their first separate experiences away from home and from one another, when they were nine, were difficult for both of them. We anticipated that this might be the case, so, the prior year, when they were eight, we signed them up for their first sleepover camp together. Nonetheless, in their separate summer camps the following year, David had terrible bouts of homesickness that he had to tolerate by himself, and Jonny had to cope with his shyness and social anxiety because he didn't have David with him to put him at ease. As difficult as these summer camp experiences were for each of our sons, I believe that it was a monumental achievement for both boys to have handled themselves alone in their respective away-from-home environments. Over the course of a few weeks, they realized that they could manage on their own.

Going away to sleepover camp signifies a major transition for elementary school–age children, whether they're singletons or twins. They are leaving home probably for the first time, which means that they don't have you to check in with at the end of their day, to console them when something goes wrong, and to provide instantaneous emotional comfort. To feel secure enough within oneself to be away from your parents for a week or more requires a high degree of emotional maturity, and the process of maturation happens in stages. It's important to remember that each child reaches these stages at his or her own pace. Sleepovers at friends' houses, going off to day camp, and attending other away-from-home activities are preliminary steps toward being able to separate from one's parents for a longer time.

For twins, there is also the question of being ready to separate from one's same-age sibling for more than a few hours or a few days. As we discussed earlier with regard to separate classrooms, if one or both twins don't seem ready to go off to separate sleepover camps, you can help one or both of them transition into readiness gradually. You might first send them to separate day camps, for example, so that the following summer they'll be ready for a more extended separation. Remember, too, that one twin might be more independent and prepared for her separate camp experience than the other. I know of a mom who signed up one seven-year-old twin for a day camp that involved a half-hour bus ride, while the other twin attended a day camp at her nearby school where she was familiar with the kids and the environment. A parent of ten-year-old twin boys decided to send her more independent son to sleepover camp for a month, while the other boy attended for just two weeks. Again, the key is to respect each child's individuality, which includes each one's individual readiness for a separate summer camp experience.

Sometimes our anxiety as parents makes it difficult for us to offer challenging experiences for our children that promote their inner growth, such as going away to camp without their twin. In our attempt to minimize their emotional discomfort, we too often hesitate to provide age-appropriate tasks, and we thereby communicate to our kids our lack of confidence in them. Some twins may grow up believing that they can't manage new situations without each other. They feel unable to master new challenges on their own. If twins assume that they always require each other to survive life experiences, they might find it difficult to engage in separate activities or relationships and will likely be overwhelmed and ill equipped when they're presented with the chance to do so. Twins need to know that they can be alone, without their twin, and are capable of making friends, being appreciated as an individual, and feeling strong in their singularity. We can help each child know this by giving him the opportunity to join a soccer team or go off to camp on his own and prove to himself that he can handle it.

Parents-of-Twins Journal: Elementary School

WRITE DOWN YOUR THOUGHTS

- If your twins have never been separated, how do you feel about their entering separate classes in kindergarten?
- If your twins are older than kindergarten age, how did they initially adjust to being in separate classes? How did this make you feel?
- How do you feel about the academic, social, and emotional differences between your twins? How do they feel about those differences?
- When other kids focus on "the twin thing," how do your twins react? How do you help them deal with this?

Tips for Parents of Elementary School–Age Twins

- Allow each child to gravitate to what interests him, assuring him that his and his twin's interests might be similar or different. Let each one choose the after-school activities he'd like to get involved with, and be supportive of those choices.

- Don't allow your discomfort over "unequal" treatment of your twins to prevent you from disciplining one and not the other when such discipline is warranted. Failure to provide consequences for your child's unacceptable behavior will result in his increasing inability to control his emotions and actions.

- Let each child know that you respect her best efforts at school. Don't compare her report card with her twin's.

- Appreciate that sibling rivalry is normal for twins as well as singletons, and don't expect your same-age siblings necessarily to be best friends.

- If both twins are ready for a separate camp experience but both want to go to the same camp, sign them up for different sessions.

- Give elementary school–age twins as much emotional and physical space as possible. If they can't have their own rooms, provide space for individual expression within their shared room.

• seven •

PRETEENS AND TEENS

Tessa is much prettier than me. She got her period and wears a bra, and I'm just this flat-chested nothing. She doesn't like to go to the mall together anymore since she has girlfriends she'd rather go with. She doesn't actually say she likes them better than me, but I know she does because she always has a different excuse. I don't even feel like we're twins anymore.

—LIANNE, THIRTEEN, TESSA'S TWIN SISTER

I still consider Lianne my closest friend, but I'm starting to have more of my own friends now. We do things together where Lianne wouldn't really fit in. I feel bad, though, because I don't want her to feel left out.

—TESSA, THIRTEEN, LIANNE'S TWIN SISTER

Adolescence is a time when young people seek to pull away from their parents in order to forge an identity that reflects their own preferences and values. Preteens and teens come to realize that their parents don't know them as well as they think they do and that they're sometimes wrong about other things as well. While adolescents want to create a sense of self separate from their parents, they also feel the need to identify closely with others who can relate to their developing personas, which is why teenagers and preteenagers usually feel most comfortable when they're part of a peer group whose members share their interests and tastes.

How do twins adapt to a developmental agenda that calls for separation from parents, identification with peers, and, most importantly, the creation of an individual identity? Being seen as a similar, identical, or cute "twosome" generally loses its appeal during adolescence. Other teens often regard twins who appear too closely connected as weird, freaky, or uncool. And twins themselves, even if they didn't before, often want to distinguish themselves from their same-age sibling. Still, these are generalizations. Many twins at this age continue to define themselves in terms of their twinship and continue to want to be more closely connected to their same-age sibling than to anyone else.

How each twin navigates through the preteen and teenage years depends upon how parents have conceptualized the twinship and treated each child up to this point. If twins have been treated as a unit, their efforts at separateness will likely take different paths than if each one has always been encouraged to be his or her own person. In this chapter, we'll consider the issue of adolescent individuation from a twin perspective and discover that there is more than one way to establish an identity that's separate from one's twin. Some avenues to individuality can be troubling or unhealthy, such as when one twin engages in dangerous behavior or becomes anorexic in order to stand apart from her twin. We will talk about how you can intervene to prevent and deal with such behaviors.

We'll also discuss how you can help your preteen and teenage twins cope with physical differences between them, which can be particularly distressing to kids at this age. Like Lianne, some twins may have a hard time accepting that their same-age sibling is developing physically at a faster rate and has thus gained entry into a teen world from which they feel shut out. We'll explore the issue of popularity and how parents can sensitively handle the situation when one twin is more social than the other. And when it's time to fill out college applications, still more sensitivity is required as parents of twins face the expectable academic and social discrepancies between their same-age children. Finally, we will discuss the issue of twin separation anxiety as twin teens look forward to college and their new lives as young adults.

Rebelling against the Twinship

When we think of teen rebellion, we generally picture kids rebelling against their parents or other adult authority figures. The normal developmental drive to become independent from one's parents may take the form of wild fashion choices, adversarial language and opinions, uncharacteristic choices in friends, or bizarre behavior that's certain to displease mom and dad. Each of these actions represents an attempt to strike out on one's own and create an identity that's clearly separate from one's parents.

For twins, another form of rebellion may emerge during the preteen and teen years: rebellion against being a twin. It's not hard to understand why adolescent twins would feel the need to distinguish themselves from their same-age sibling at this point in their lives. During these years, kids seek to define themselves as individuals and at the same time gain acceptance from their friends. If same-age siblings pretty much stick together at school and during social activities, others often relate to them as a duo. While a twosome is frequently showered with celebritylike attention in elementary school, in the eyes of teen peers, twins who come off as being too alike or too close may be deemed socially unacceptable. So, twins at this stage are often motivated to downplay the twin dynamic. Sometimes they do so by sporting a look that's the polar opposite of their twin's or by acting in an extreme opposite manner to their same-age sibling. If one twin dresses like a jock, the other might go goth. If one twin is involved in student government, the other might avoid student activities and start a garage band or hang out with the "bad" crowd simply to distinguish herself from her twin.

The need to cause a dramatic break in the twin relationship is usually the result of twins' not having been encouraged, or given the chance, to develop their individuality earlier in their lives. In the case of one twin's turning to the bad crowd, the bad twin/good twin dynamic can ironically reinforce twin-dependent behavior. That's because the "good twin" often takes it upon himself to cover up the bad twin's deeds, thereby perpetuating the dependent behavior that led to the twins splitting up in the first place. Sixteen-year-old twins Lukas and Shauna's story is a case in point.

Before Shauna started hanging out with the "druggie" crowd in high school, she and Lukas had always been best friends. When they were little, their mom marveled at how they seemed to take care of each other, make each other laugh, and follow each other around. They adapted easily to preschool, she said, because they had each other as loyal playmates. Their preschool teacher remarked about how cute they were, always holding hands when it was time to line up. In grade school, they were in separate classes but looked for each other on the playground after lunch so they could play basketball together. They had a hoop at home as well, and playing one-on-one was their favorite after-school activity all through elementary and middle school. "Friends from the neighborhood would sometimes come by to join in," their mom told me, "but the twins always preferred playing on their own. They said the other kids messed it up between them. I guess they just had a thing going, the two of them. I never thought anything of it, figuring it was normal for twins to want to be together."

When they got to high school, where there were kids who hadn't known the twins in middle school, Lukas and Shauna's togetherness seemed odd to some of their classmates. Off-color comments implying that the twins' relationship was incestuous were hurled at them whenever they walked past a certain crowd. Their parents only found out about the remarks because Lukas let it slip one night at dinner. Their parental advice was simply, "Stay away from those kids, and don't let what they say get to you."

Not too long after that, Shauna began to break away from Lukas. She started wearing only black clothes and dark eye makeup, listening to music that her dad found "angry and jarring," and spending time with kids who dressed like her and, according to her mother, "had that same sad expression." Meanwhile, Lukas was busy with junior varsity basketball and a few new friends he had made on the team. He and Shauna still talked and teased each other at home, but clearly their lives had taken divergent paths.

One night Shauna came home reeking of marijuana, and her father forbade her to see the kids she'd been with that evening. Shauna screamed at him that he didn't understand how much she needed her friends. "They're the only ones who get who I really am!" she cried. Meanwhile, she continued to smoke grass and experiment with other hallucinogenic drugs. Rather than risk her parents finding her "secret stash," she prevailed upon her twin brother to keep it in his room. Lukas went along with the plan, even though he later defended himself by telling his dad, "I was trying to talk her out of taking drugs, and I thought if I helped her out at first, she would eventually listen to me."

So, once again, Lukas and Shauna had become a team, this time one whose goal was to keep Shauna's drug use from her parents. Lukas felt it was somehow his responsibility not only to help his sister out by hiding the drugs for her but also to help her overcome her drug problem. The twinship had always been the primary relationship for both Lukas and Shauna. Neither parent had established a very close connection to either twin, assuming that they were essentially taking care of each other and fulfilling each other's needs. When Shauna began heading in an unhealthy direction, Lukas was the one she confided in. And Lukas took it upon himself to try to "straighten her out," rather than enlisting the help of his parents.

I told Lukas and Shauna's parents that siblings tend to be very loyal to each other, and twins are especially loyal to one another. That loyalty is tested in adolescence because teens often keep secrets from their parents as they seek to become more independent and experiment with new behaviors. Telling one's parents about your twin's drug use would mean siding with "the enemy" in order to expose the person you're closest to. In addition, Lukas was acting in a quasiparental role by believing he could somehow "fix" Shauna's behavior. But it's not healthy for twins to parent each other, and this is especially true in adolescence, when dangerous behavior may begin to evolve. I explained to Lukas and Shauna's parents that Lukas likely took on this role with his sister because of the tremendous responsibility that one twin often feels for the other. This sense of responsibility can be so powerful that the "parenting" twin does not consider the option of asking for help from mom or dad.

Parents need to try to be aware of what's going on with their teens. And they need to try to communicate with them so that, when serious problems beyond the young person's ability to solve on her own arise, mom or dad can recognize the situation and figure out what to do. A major challenge in parenting adolescents is knowing when your children can manage and when you need to step in to guide them and set limits. Lukas and Shauna's parents also needed to understand that Shauna might have been acting out in this way, in addition to all the normal teenage reasons, as a means of establishing her separateness and forming her singular identity.

If each twin is already comfortable with her own identity apart from her same-age sibling, she won't feel the need to rebel against being a twin. She may still act out and rebel against her parents, as many teens do, but the twinship will not be the issue. It is those who have yet to begin charting a course toward becoming their own person who use the preteen and teen years as a convenient time to break away from their twin, if only superficially.

It's one thing to dress differently from one's twin, listen to different music, or hang out with a different crowd; it's another to feel an authentic sense of independence from that twin. The longer twins have been dependent upon each other for their emotional needs, and the longer they have put off discovering who they are apart from their same-age sibling, the more difficult the process of self-discovery becomes.

Not all twins attempt to distinguish themselves from each other in such a radical manner as Shauna did. My sister and I got involved in different activities in junior high and high school, but our differences were mainly extensions of how we had always been labeled by other people. My parents and others had consistently identified me as "the outgoing, social one," so in high school I opted to be involved in numerous school activities and to be known on that score. My sister was "the smart one," and thus she chose to take college-level courses in high school, at which she excelled. Unfortunately, these superficial differences in our choice of activities did little to create any real separateness; rather, they simply added to the illusion that we were each doing our own thing. In fact, since we had never been treated as distinct individuals, we were still tied to each other in a manner that was deeply oppressive to both of us. Jane saw herself for many years as the shy, quiet, passive twin who could not compete with her louder, opinionated, powerful sister. And I found it difficult to feel deserving or happy about my accomplishments because I worried that they might make Jane feel overshadowed or envious.

While some teen twins, like Jane and me, give the impression that they are going their separate ways, others, like Shauna, veer dramatically from their same-age sibling in order to make up for lost time. Still other twin pairs do not attempt to demonstrate separateness, even during adolescence, because separating in any way is simply too unbearable for them and their families to contemplate. It is often these twins who go off to college together, perhaps living together as roommates, unable to consider independent paths. They may rationalize their decision by telling themselves that a college campus will be big enough to offer each of them a separate experience, but their choice to remain together most likely means that they're still tied to one another emotionally. Of course, twins who are emotionally healthy feel less need either to stick together or to rebel against the twinship because they have been raised to think of themselves as separate individuals who will chart their futures independently of the other.

How can you tell if one or both of your twins is rebelling against the twinship or merely expressing the expected teen rebellion against parental authority? If you've encouraged your children throughout their childhood to pursue their own interests and have their own friendships, and if you have treated each child as an individual rather than as half of "the twins," they probably won't have the need as teenagers to prove themselves as separate from their twin. Each will already be living proof of his or her individuality. If, on the other hand, your twins have always been treated as a duo and have been overly reliant on one another, and they now seem to be acting out the previously suppressed desire to be separate and unique, they may need your support in separating from each other in a healthy way. It's not too late to spend some consistent alone time with each one to learn more about the individual person each is struggling to become.

Fat Twin, Thin Twin

Comparison and competition are virtually impossible to avoid, especially for twins. A twin frequently grows up being judged in relationship to her same-age sibling rather than on her own terms. Childhood can be a constant battle to prove her worthiness and singularity. And if her parents can't seem to relate to her as an individual, during adolescence she may try to gain mom and dad's or peers' attention through desperate measures. Whatever it takes, she'll struggle to get her parents and others to perceive her as separate from, and perhaps more worthy than, her same-age sibling. Sometimes, in extreme cases, this can take a very dramatic form. Here's what fourteen-year-old Monique decided to do.

Monique and her twin sister, Paulina, had a mother who related to them only as "the girls" or "the twins." She took pride in her daughters' achievements but never passed up an opportunity to compare one to the other. She couldn't seem to finish a sentence about one girl's successes or struggles without bringing up the other girl's performance in the same arena. Both girls were athletic in their own ways, but instead of appreciating each one's unique talents, their mom seemed to turn every victory for one into a defeat for the other. She would say things like, "Paulina is a natural at gymnastics, but Monique can barely do a somersault!" or, "Monique scored the final point in their basketball game, but poor Paulina never got off the bench."

Both girls were slightly overweight when they entered puberty, but in their last year of middle school, Paulina started dieting. She didn't discuss it with Monique, but Monique couldn't help but notice. "I saw that she'd take smaller portions at dinner, and she wouldn't snack on cookies or ice cream at night like we used to," Monique told me. "Then, after a few months, it seemed like all of a sudden she was thin and I was fat. I hated that. I couldn't stand being 'the fat twin.'" Monique decided she would eat even less than Paulina. Not only would she forego the cookies and snacks, but she would give up eating altogether. At her thinnest, Monique weighed less than ninety pounds.

While some aspects of Monique's anorexia related to competition with her sister for the distinction of "thinnest," it was also about distinguishing herself from Paulina. She had created a unique identity as the waifish, sickly twin who needed extra attention from her parents to help her out of the unhealthy predicament she'd fallen into. Confused about who she was apart from her sister and stymied by ambivalence over wanting to be separate from her twin, Monique chose to control the only thing she could: her food intake.

As a parent, it is crucial to avoid comparing your same-age siblings, just as you would avoid judging one singleton against another. Every child deserves to be acknowledged and respected for her uniqueness, and teenagers are especially sensitive about being perceived as uniquely their own person. Given how often twins are compared to each other in the outside world, you can appreciate their need for your validation as individuals, especially at this important turning point in their lives. Do them that honor, and they will be much more likely to develop a strong sense of self-awareness and self-respect, attributes that are far more important than the ideal body weight.

One Shaves, One Doesn't

It's hard enough when your best friend gets her first bra, and you're months away from needing one. Or your best buddy got a shaving kit for his twelfth birthday, and at thirteen and a half you're still waiting for facial fuzz to appear. When you're a twin and your same-age, same-sex sibling shows obvious physical signs of being more mature than you are, it can be even more devastating. "How can we be twins when she's already wearing a 32B and I don't even need a training bra!" your daughter might ask. As parents of preteen or teen twins, you'll need to be able to answer such questions. Needing a bra or a shave may seem like superficial concerns when compared with academic achievement or social success, but to the adolescent who is waiting to "catch up" to his or her twin, they're important matters.

Sometimes, as in the case of Lianne and Tessa, the teen who is more physically mature breaks away from her twin at the same time that their physical differences are most apparent. This may be pure coincidence, or it may not. When one teen looks older, she may not want to hang out with her more childish-looking twin. Her more womanly physical appearance can make her feel emotionally older and more mature, even if that's not the case. It was clear that Tessa had mixed feelings about spending more time with her own friends. On the one hand, she was happy to hang out with kids who accepted her on her own terms; on the other, she was worried about Lianne's feeling left out. The two had always considered themselves to be best friends and only recently had begun to have separate social lives. But Lianne was still feeling her way socially, while Tessa seemed to have found her niche with a particular group of girls. Still, Tessa felt twinges of guilt about it, and the physical differences between her and Lianne only added to the growing division between them. To her credit, Tessa opted to stick with her new friends rather than caving in to feelings of guilt—which left Lianne to cope with a sense of loss and inadequacy.

After she and I discussed how best to handle Lianne's upset feelings, the twins' mom told me that she had a talk with Lianne in which she let her know that feeling sad and angry about not spending as much time with Tessa was to be expected. After all, they had been each other's closest friend since they were little, and it was understandable that Lianne might feel rejected by her sister. Sometimes not being included in your twin's new circle of friends can feel like you're being "dumped" because the most important person in your life no longer finds you as important. Lianne's mom assured Lianne that she and Tessa would still be friends, just not as exclusively as they once were. She told her that making new friends would be a challenge since no one would know her as well as her twin sister had, but she encouraged Lianne to begin making plans with other girls so she wouldn't feel so left out of Tessa's new social life.

Her mom also shared with Lianne that when she was a girl, she had not gotten her period or her first bra until she was almost fourteen. While other girls were filling out their bikinis, Lianne's mom had worn a baggy T-shirt over hers to cover up what she didn't yet have. She promised Lianne that her time would come. In the meantime, the two of them went to the mall together, where Lianne picked out a soft pink bralette with spaghetti straps and a new pink lip gloss. The bra and lip gloss lifted Lianne's spirits, as did the time alone with her mom.

As a parent, how do you deal with an adolescent who feels he is less mature or less valuable than his twin due to physical differences? A girl or boy whose same-sex twin is more physically developed will need your understanding and encouragement. You might try having a conversation like this one:

YOU: Why so down?

YOUR TEEN: I'm not down.

YOU: I can tell something's bothering you.

YOUR TEEN: Why is he already shaving when I'm not?

YOU: Twins don't necessarily go through puberty at exactly the same time.

YOUR TEEN: So, if he's going through puberty and I'm not, that means he's more mature, right?

YOU: Not really. He's physically more developed, but that's not what maturity is about.

YOUR TEEN: Girls think it is.

YOU: Not all girls. Not everyone judges people by how they look. Besides, you're a good-looking guy, and you'll get hair on your face one of these days; trust me.

YOUR TEEN: Soon?

YOU: Soon enough . . . and if you take after me, you may even be hairier than your brother.

YOUR TEEN: Not funny, Dad. I don't want to be hairy. I just want to shave.

YOU: You will. I promise.

Academic Differences and College Plans: Two Very Different Stories

The parents of seventeen-year-old twin girls Lucy and Stephanie came to see me after a traumatic event at the girls' progressive private high school. The sisters were juniors, and the parents had been called in to discuss academic options with the school counselor, whose framed diploma revealed that she was a graduate of an Ivy League university. The twin sisters were both present at the meeting, as requested by the counselor. It seems that Lucy had a 3.7 grade point average, and Stephanie had a 2.8. Since the purpose of the meeting was to discuss which schools would be the best options based on each girl's grade point average, as well as other factors, the counselor began to suggest various schools for which each would be best suited.

With such a wide disparity in their grades, Lucy's potential choices were very different from Stephanie's. As the counselor began to discuss which schools each girl might consider applying to, Stephanie suddenly burst into tears. Lucy and her mother rushed to Stephanie, threw their arms around her, and tried to soothe her. But Stephanie burst out, "I'm so sorry! I've ruined it. . . . Because my grades are so low, now we can't go to the same school!"

The counselor appeared to be taken aback by Stephanie's outburst, the parents were distressed that Lucy and Stephanie would have to face the next phase of their education on their own, and both girls were so upset by the news that they'd likely be separating the following year that neither could focus on the options being discussed. What was wrong with this picture?

In my view, it was a stunning miscalculation for the school counselor to have called in the girls together. Why had she assumed that two students should be counseled at the same time, even if they were sisters who happened to be the same age? Hadn't she anticipated that Stephanie might feel humiliated when her lower grades were discussed in the context of her sister's higher ones? This was an Ivy League–educated counselor, yet she clearly had no understanding of how twins need to be treated as separate individuals. To her credit, she seemed to have acknowledged the error of her ways when she remarked afterwards to the girls' mother, "I'm sorry to have upset your daughters. I should have called them in separately. I just always think of twins as wanting to be together."

As for the parents, if they had known that the meeting was for the purpose of discussing academic options for their daughters, they should have made sure that each girl had the chance to meet with the counselor separately. One girl's academic history and future options don't involve her sister. However, it was obvious that the parents' thinking was not unlike the counselor's and that the twin mystique had been a guiding principle in their parenting decisions. Throughout their daughters' childhoods, they had encouraged them to stick together, failed to encourage them to pursue separate experiences, and had thoroughly bought into the notion that twinship togetherness is forever—or at least extends into college and beyond.

The girls would not have been so heartsick at not being able to go to the same college had they become accustomed to and enjoyed being apart from each other at times throughout their childhood. Never having done so, at the age of seventeen, they faced the prospect of separation with a sense of panic and dread. When they got home from school that evening, Lucy told her parents, "I don't care about going to the schools the counselor recommended! It doesn't matter to me at all. It's much more important that Steph and I stay together."

I told Stephanie and Lucy's parents that this crisis was clearly about the girls' anxiety about separating from each other, which they needed to address with their daughters. Although the girls and their parents had known all along that Lucy consistently earned higher grades than Stephanie, they had all been avoiding the subject of the sisters' eventual need to separate. The girls had always been together in school, and one sister rarely did anything socially without the other. As for the possibility of going off to different colleges one day, the parents had never discussed with their daughters what it might be like for them not to be with one another. Understandably, that's what each girl was terribly frightened about.

I suggested that Lucy and Stephanie's parents talk to their daughters and tell them something like this:

> *We realize that going off to separate colleges is going to be difficult for you, but each of you needs to be at the college that's right for you. We want you to know that, as parents, we have made mistakes. We should have addressed the issue of pursuing your own individual goals and leading separate lives much sooner. But we know you will be able to handle it. And maybe a good way of learning to be apart in college would be to separate from each other for a month this summer, so you can get a sense of what it's going to be like. So, maybe you, Lucy, could do a month of community service somewhere away from home, which you've told us you might enjoy doing. And, Stephanie, you could get that job at the boutique that you were trying to talk Lucy into working at with you. After that month, you'll still have some time to spend together before you leave for college.*

It won't be easy being without each other, but we're going to get you a cell phone plan so you can talk to each other as much as you want. You'll be able to tell each other about the new experiences you're having, which you may not have been able to have as a twosome. As much as you'll miss each other, this will be a new beginning for each of you. And in the long run, you'll benefit from it. The older you get, the harder it will be to separate, so it's time you each had the chance to have your own life.

Every twin needs to experience being out in the world as a singleton. If a young person has not been responded to as someone other than a twin, she will be unprepared to deal with a separate life as an adult. She will not know what it's like to experience herself as an individual, to know who she is apart from her sister. So, it's important to help your teens face their separation anxiety realistically. Let them know they can expect to have periods of missing their twin and that that's okay. They may experience a sense of grief and loss, maybe even the feeling that they can't get along without their twin; if that's the case, they may want to talk to a therapist about what they're going through and what they're feeling. They should understand that such reactions to being apart from each other are neither freakish nor unusual but absolutely understandable given that they've never been separated before. They should also expect, however, that over time they will overcome their anxiety and sadness about separating from each other. And they will value and take pride in their individuality.

A second story offers an entirely different picture of how twins can handle the academic differences between them, as well as the prospect of going away to different colleges, when they've been raised with the philosophy that each child is his own separate person.

Kevin and Adam's parents were aware early on that Adam was more scholastically oriented than Kevin. Even in preschool, Adam gravitated toward picture books and writing exercises. He also loved to draw. Kevin enjoyed more active pursuits, like seeing how fast he could make it up the ladder and down the slide. He was slow to learn his letters and numbers, but he was good at any game that involved running around; team tag was his favorite. In elementary school, Kevin excelled in sports; he also had an interest in anything having to do with animals. Biological science was the one subject he often got Bs in. Throughout elementary school, it became apparent that Adam's grades were always going to be higher than Kevin's. He was tested and rated as "gifted" and placed in special classes whenever those were made available.

When he reached middle school, Adam's parents enrolled him in a special school for gifted students, and by the time he was in high school, he began to take college courses as part of his curriculum. He consistently earned As, had a wide range of academic interests, and was considering either architecture or international relations. He would clearly have his pick of a number of top-notch universities. Kevin, meanwhile, attended public school and continued to earn mostly Cs and Bs. He was also on the track team and had an ongoing interest in karate—and animals. His high school counselor suggested that he might start out at a community college, perhaps as a biology major, and then transfer to a state university. Kevin was considering either becoming a vet or eventually starting his own pet care business.

Throughout their educational careers, Kevin and Adam's parents encouraged each boy to pursue what he enjoyed and to challenge himself at what he was most interested in. They also made it a point not to compare one twin with the other. They enthusiastically commended Kevin on his science projects, even when he only earned a C+, because they could tell he was passionate about animal rights, animal habitats, and animal behavior. Adam's successes were, of course, also praised, but never more than Kevin's. Their dad told me, "For Kevin to put his heart and soul into a report on polar bears and get a C+ was as impressive to us as Adam getting an A in a college-level sociology course. As long as they're both excited about what they're involved in, that's what it's all about."

With such an attitude on the part of their father, it's no wonder that Kevin didn't feel threatened or diminished by Adam's outstanding accomplishments and that Adam acknowledged what his brother was accomplishing as well. The brothers took their differences for granted but also enjoyed the many things they had in common: a love of the beach and bodysurfing, watching horror movies, and a fanatic devotion to barbequed ribs, to name just a few. Even though they had been at separate schools since they were twelve, Kevin and Adam had always been good friends. When they headed off to different college campuses, they would definitely miss each other, but they wouldn't need each other in order to feel confident or complete.

The Most Popular Twin

When our sons were in their early teens, David's friends would often call him to get together—to go to the park or the movies or a party—and at times David didn't go out with them because he felt badly that Jonny wasn't included. We didn't realize that this was happening, that David was turning down his friends in order to prevent Jonny from feeling left out. It was our older daughters who eventually told us what was going on. My husband and I encouraged David to be with his friends when he wanted to. We explained to him that it was not his responsibility to take care of Jonny, that Jonny could handle his brother's going places without him. And even if Jonny did feel left out, he would be okay. Adjusting to the differences between him and David, including differences in their social lives, was part of the challenge of being a twin. In fact, Jonny had his own friends, just not as many as David had.

Jonny has a different personality than David, and his social life is also different. As I mentioned earlier, Jonny tended to keep the several close friends he made in elementary school because he seems to appreciate loyalty and the deepening of sophisticated friendships over the years. David was constantly branching out and making new friends. With his outgoing, engaging personality, David seems to draw people to him naturally, which is something we hope he appreciates about himself. Still, his concern for Jonny's feelings was characteristic of the sensitivity twins often have regarding how their behavior affects their same-age sibling. As a young teen, David worried that by accepting too many social invitations, he would cause Jonny to doubt his own popularity.

Since peer group acceptance is highly valued during adolescence, the question of one twin's being "more popular" than the other can be taken pretty seriously. Twins like David can feel pangs of anxiety when their same-age sibling isn't invited to the same social events, and parents of twins wonder what they can do to lessen the sting of one teen or preteen's being "more popular" than the other. One mom so wanted her "unpopular" daughter, Michelle, to be as popular as the girl's twin brother, Ray, that she took extreme measures, which sadly backfired.

Thirteen-year-olds Michelle and Ray had never been that close. They got along well and rarely fought; they simply had very different temperaments and tastes. Both were bright and did well in school, but Ray was also a student leader and an actor in school plays. He was constantly on the phone making plans with his friends, and his weekends were spent in their company. Michelle was quiet and somewhat withdrawn, preferring to spend her free time either taking long bike rides or holed up in her room reading novels and writing in her journal. In the spring, she participated on a Little League softball team, but she rarely got together with any of the girls outside of the official practices and games.

Michelle and Ray's divergent social lives did not seem to be much of a problem until the two were in their last year of middle school and their mother began to pressure Michelle to make friends. "I just didn't think it was healthy for Michelle to be off on her own so much of the time," her mom told me. "And I couldn't understand how she could be the mirror opposite of her brother—and of me. I was always one of the most popular girls in high school, and I wanted Michelle to experience the kind of fun that I had. You only get one chance to enjoy your high school years, and I felt like Michelle wasn't going to be prepared to enjoy hers."

Taking matters into her own hands without consulting either of her kids, Michelle and Ray's mom decided to buy expensive tickets to a rock concert, telling the twins that they could each invite three friends. Ray had no problem choosing which friends to invite, but Michelle told her mom she didn't want to go. "I like the band, but I had no one to invite, and I didn't want to go with Ray and his friends," Michelle told me. Rather than accept Michelle's wishes, her mom used the list of girls on Michelle's softball team and called the three she thought Michelle knew best. Of course, the girls were thrilled to be invited to the concert since the seats were in the best section, and the band was everyone's favorite.

Michelle was humiliated that her mom had gone behind her back and invited girls she hardly knew. At the concert, the other three girls chatted among themselves, barely speaking to Michelle, who was too shy to join in their conversations. Ray and his friends were either talking to each other or flirting with the three girls from Michelle's team. When they got home that night, Michelle ran up to her room and slammed the door without saying goodnight to anyone. Her mom couldn't understand why Michelle hadn't enjoyed herself. "I don't get why she can't at least make the effort," she complained to me later in my office.

Michelle's mom had violated every tenet of adolescence, namely, not to be intruded upon, not to be told how to behave, and not to be coached on whom to choose as friends. An extrovert herself, Michelle's mother couldn't accept that Michelle enjoyed being by herself, writing poems in her journal, and reading novels. It was inconceivable to this mom that Michelle could be so strikingly different from her and from Michelle's twin brother. Ensuring her daughter's popularity was far more important than respecting the girl's choices and decisions. Sadly, this mom's inability to accept the differences between her son and her daughter meant that she didn't really accept or respect who her daughter really was.

I tried to convey to Michelle's mom that she needed to recognize that each of her children approached life differently, and one approach was not necessarily better than the other. They were just different kids. It was important that she allow Michelle to be her own person, rather than insisting that she be more like her brother—and more like she herself was in high school. This mom also needed to think about why she preferred Ray to Michelle. Maybe from the time they were born, she had a preference for Ray because his gregariousness was more like her own personality, and Michelle's shy personality made her feel uncomfortable. Some kids just aren't that social—and that should be okay. I encouraged Michelle's mom to think about Michelle in her own light, rather than comparing her to Ray. I also told her that it's not unusual for adolescents to want to be off on their own at times and that this inclination shouldn't necessarily be interpreted as being antisocial. If Michelle felt that she was entitled to make her own choices without the interference of her mother or the constant comparison to her brother's popularity, chances were she would reach out to those friends she felt were right for her.

Most of us can't help but feel for the teen who doesn't seem to attract friends the way his or her twin so easily does. So, what does a well-intentioned parent do when one twin is popular and the other isn't? It may be more helpful to understand what not to do.

- Don't pressure your teen to be more like her twin by forcing her to attend social events or to invite friends over. At this age, young people need to begin to manage their own social lives. By interfering or pressuring her, you'll be sending the signal that she's not competent enough to make her own friends.

- Don't expect, require, or encourage one twin to include the other in social activities. It will not only thwart both twins from developing their own friendships, but it may result in other kids not wanting to include either twin in future plans.

- Don't feel sorry for the twin who is less popular than his brother or sister. Your sense of pity or worry will only make your teen feel worse. Treat social-life differences between your twins the same as you treat other same-age sibling differences: with acceptance.

- Don't buy into the adolescent concept that popularity is all-important. Happiness and success in life aren't necessarily about popularity. A few close friends are more rewarding than a flock of fans. And often it's the teenage "loners" who grow up to be the most creative and most accomplished individuals.

- On the other hand, don't diminish the importance of your popular twin's likeability in order to make the other twin feel better. To be genuinely friendly and easygoing, to have a great sense of humor or a "fun-to-be-with" personality—each of these are wonderful qualities. If one twin possesses them and the other doesn't, that's okay.

As with all differences between twins, the key is to make sure you convey to your kids that each possesses his or her own unique traits, strengths, and talents. Being a twin does not mean that you're doomed to live in a constant state of comparison and competition. If you encourage each child to value his own abilities and to work on those he hopes to strengthen, and if you remember to tell each teen how much you appreciate his positive attributes, the less-popular twin will likely be able to congratulate his brother for being voted "Most Popular" on the senior poll without feeling inferior. And the popular twin will allow himself to enjoy his sociability without feeling guilty.

Parents-of-Twins Journal: Preteens and Teens

WRITE DOWN YOUR THOUGHTS

- In what ways does each twin reveal his or her individuality? How does this make the other twin feel? How does it make you feel?
- If one twin is maturing physically at a faster rate than the other, how might you help each one to feel comfortable about their physical differences?
- How do you and your spouse spend alone time with each of your preteens or teens? What have you learned about each child during these times?
- How do you handle differences between your twins when it comes to academics, social life, and temperament?
- As they approach high school graduation, how prepared are your twins to lead happy and fulfilling lives apart from each other?

Tips for Parents of
Preteen and Teenage Twins

- If your adolescent twins have not had much opportunity to be away from each other, help them organize some separate activities so that they can begin to have experiences where they're not related to as "so and so's twin."

- If your twins' effort to individuate from each other becomes too difficult, offer them the option of attending separate schools.

- Although it may be harder to arrange as they get older, continue to spend "alone time" with each twin. Sporting events, shopping, and driving them to lessons or social activities (before they're driving themselves) can provide such opportunities.

- It's not too late to sign up your preteen or teen twins for separate summer activities. The experience will help each to develop self-assurance and a sense of independence from the other.

- Understand that it's okay for twins to engage in similar activities if these really reflect their true interests. Don't make one twin feel that he has to choose something different from his twin in order to prove his individuality.

- Be aware of one twin's making sacrifices for the other, and let both twins know that this is not expected or necessary. Continue to support the notion that each will be invited to do things without the other and that learning to adjust to having separate lives is part of growing up.

- Don't ask one twin to clue you in about the other's behavior. If you suspect that one teen is involved in unhealthy or dangerous behavior, go to the source and discuss your concerns with that child. It's your job to find out what's going on with your kids; it's not the responsibility of one twin to inform on the other.

- Talk about the future with your high school–age twins, letting them know that you don't assume they will go to the same college or stay together as they mature. If they do decide on the same college, let them know that you don't think it's a good idea for them to be roommates.

• eight •

TWO YOUNG ADULTS

I was so nervous about Veronica coming to visit me and Paul because I didn't want her to feel displaced. I had always wished that she would be the one to meet someone first because I felt that I could handle the jealously and rejection and resentment a lot better than she could. You know those lonely, awkward feelings that you get with girlfriends when they have a boyfriend and you are excluded from their lives? Well, with twins it's exaggerated tenfold. I told Paul that Veronica had always been the number-one person in my life. So, I was really nervous anticipating how the three of us would get along.

—MEGAN, TWENTY–FIVE–YEAR–OLD
TWIN SISTER OF VERONICA

B y the time your twins reach young adulthood, you may feel that your job as a parent is completed. But there will still be times when you'll be called upon to give advice to one or the other of your twins as they struggle to adjust to adult life. Whether it's relationship problems, career concerns, or existential dilemmas, if you have a close connection to each of your young-adult children, they will likely come to you for your guidance and input. And knowing how to help them handle those issues that specifically relate to their twinship will be enormously valuable.

As a group leader and psychotherapist for twins and their parents, I have found that parents long to know how their twins are going to turn out as adults. Will they still be close? Will they discover their place in the world without the aid or influence of their same-age sibling? Will they find a love relationship that is as close as their twinship? Sometimes parents are frightened by media stories about inseparable twins who always dress alike, who live together and never marry, and who even isolate themselves from the outside world. Of course, this is not what parents want for their children, but they also don't want their twins to lose the close connection they have forged over the years.

In this chapter, we're going to hear from various adult twins whose lives reflect the parenting philosophies under which they were brought up. Several duos have separated geographically but not emotionally, and thus each sibling continues to need the other and to define himself or herself in relation to his or her twin. Other twins who share their stories here had a difficult time discovering their individuality and creating separate lives, but they are now on the path toward emotional independence.

If you practice the parenting philosophy outlined in this book, chances are your twins will manage to choose the life paths that fit their individual values and personalities, at the same time remaining close friends. While not abandoning their unique friendship, each will be able to create a satisfying life for herself, one that reflects her unique dreams and goals. She will feel free to choose a partner without being concerned that her same-age sibling might suffer from jealousy or loneliness. Whether she lives in the same town or across the country from her twin, she will undoubtedly miss seeing her as often as she did when the two were growing up, but she won't need her twin in order to lead a happy, fulfilling life.

First let's meet Megan and Veronica. At twenty-five, they are still struggling with twin issues, although both are now determined to confront them.

I'm Afraid No One Will Love Me as Much as She Does

Megan and Veronica were extremely close growing up. They have an older sister, but neither of them was particularly interested in being with her when they were younger. The two were each other's favorite playmate and best friend throughout their school years, each felt that the other knew her better than she knew herself, and they treasured their all-encompassing relationship. They also took it for granted. Only recently have they begun to reflect on the impact being a twin has had on their lives. Veronica's decision to become a school counselor prompted her to delve more deeply into her past and to ask her parents if they remembered any unusual incidents that might have related to the girls' twinship. Her mother helped Veronica recall a traumatic event that took place in the summer prior to the girls' entering second grade. She and Megan had never been separated and were about to be placed in separate classes. (Their private school had only one first-grade but two second-grade classrooms.) With her current knowledge of child development, Veronica recognized that the event was a classic example of separation anxiety. As I explained to her, however, Veronica's particular manifestation of separation anxiety also related to being a twin.

Seven-year-old Veronica had experienced what could be described as panic attacks every time her mother got ready to go out somewhere. She would whimper or cry, pleading with her mom not to leave her. It seems Veronica was terribly afraid that her mother was going to be killed in an accident or that she, Veronica, would be kidnapped and never see her mother again, never be able to say good-bye to her. When such an outburst would occur, Veronica couldn't be comforted by her father or her older sister, only by her mother or by Megan. She would cry out, "I only want mommy—or Megan!"

Why was Veronica having panic attacks at this particular point in her life? She had never had a history of relying on her mother, so why was she so afraid when her mother left the house? The panic attacks had to do with the fact that Veronica's sense of safety was based on being with her sister, and that safety was about to be threatened when the twin sisters entered separate second-grade classrooms. Veronica became profoundly worried about whom she was going to rely on.

Singleton children often experience separation anxiety when they first go to preschool or kindergarten, but Veronica and Megan had never had to go through that developmental hurdle because they had always had each other. Being in separate classes would mean they would have to face being alone for the first time. And Veronica was more panicked about that prospect than Megan.

A twin who is going through twin separation anxiety needs to have a parental figure to connect with. Spending alone time with a parent, as opposed to relying on one's twin, helps the twin understand that the person she comes to for emotional support is the parent. So, this crisis was actually a positive thing because it gave Veronica's mother an opportunity to strengthen her attachment to her daughter. As I've stressed earlier, children's primary connection needs to be with their parents. It is her parents, not her sibling, who help a child get through situations such as learning to be on one's own at school. Children have to know that their parents are the ones in control, that mom and dad can be relied on to help with issues kids are struggling with.

Alarmed by their daughter's anxiety, Veronica's parents got professional help and were counseled to spend alone time with Veronica. Her mother made every effort to do so, and by the time Veronica started the second grade, her panic attacks had subsided—but not her dependence on Megan. Even when they weren't placed in the same classroom, the twin sisters checked in with each other at school constantly, chatting about how they felt about what had happened that day and what decisions each should make.

In her recent discussions with her parents, Veronica also found out that they understood her "rebel" phase in high school—wearing grunge clothes, smoking marijuana, and hanging out with her artsy bohemian friends—as a sign that she needed to separate from Megan. "I had no idea at seventeen why I was acting out like that, but apparently my parents did." And so did Megan, who recalled that Veronica had "separated herself from the cheerleader, goody-two-shoes image that I never tried to avoid. She had to be different from me some-how." As I discussed in the last chapter, when twins don't have the opportunity to develop their individuality authentically, they often go to extremes, especially in adolescence, to prove how different they are from their same-age sibling. Even if both twins enjoy the same activity or share the same inclinations, one may choose to engage in behavior at the extreme opposite end of the spectrum, like Veronica's becoming more "bohemian" in order to distinguish herself from her "goody-two-shoes" sister, Megan.

Megan told me that she and Veronica had always taken care of one another in different ways. Megan had been the practical one. "In high school, I set the alarm, made the lunches, and drove us to volleyball practice because Veronica doesn't like to drive." And, according to Megan, Veronica had been the emotional caretaker, "except in high school and the first years of college when Veronica struggled to find out who she was and what career she wanted to pursue. I think Veronica needed me more at that time because she was unsure of herself and insecure about her future." Still, in general, Megan said that Veronica had always been the nurturer, attuned to other people's feelings, which was why she was happy to have found a career in which she could channel those innate strengths.

The sisters attended the same college, and shortly before they graduated, Megan wrote a personal narrative for a creative writing class. In the piece, Megan revealed how her closeness to Veronica had affected her own ability to be in a love relationship. The assignment was to write about your most personal fears; Megan focused on the raw emotions she felt as she anticipated living apart from her sister for the first time in her life. Here are some brief excerpts:

> "After a few dates it falls apart. He doesn't know me like she does, doesn't know what love is to me."

> "My father's suggestion that my sister and I are too close and that our closeness keeps either of us from falling in love shakes me under my skin."

> "I don't know myself without her."

> "I am afraid to be alone."

> "Veronica and I agreed to get away from each other. We need to know what the world is without each other."

> "I don't know why I'm dumping her when she and I work so well together."

> "She knows me better than I know myself."

> "I can't find it—where I stop and she begins."

> "How can I tell anyone that I feel totally incapable of loving anyone except my sister? I must be some kind of freak."

> "I decided that finding a boyfriend before Veronica left town would allow me to let her go."

The last line introduces an episode in which Megan attempts to "replace" Veronica, who was about to head off to another city after the girls' college graduation. It is achingly clear in this scenario that, although Megan realizes she must loosen the tie that has always bound her to the person she most loves in the world, it will be the most difficult thing she has ever done.

I decided that finding a boyfriend before Veronica left town would allow me to let her go. Replacing Veronica must be about the bedroom and the thing I've never done. Letting someone in must mean that I let him into my body and then he can be in my life. Then someone else can matter in my life. It's okay though, because now I understand.

I pick someone. We go out. I get drunk. I will let this one in my body. I will let him matter in my life. Still, things don't go the way they're supposed to. In bed I tell him it's okay that I've never done this before. And I think, "This is how it works." I need this to be how it works. But it doesn't work.

He stops because I'm drunk. He stops because I've never done this before. He stops because he doesn't want to matter in my life. He stops and I'm never going to know how to love somebody.

He stops calling and so do I.

I can't replace her.

I'm afraid no one will love me as much as she does.

"Veronica!" I call out to her in the midst of my retching. I shiver and sweat and cling to the toilet.

For comfort, I press my face to the bathroom floor. I crawl down the hall to my room. My roommate asks what I need, and all I say is "Veronica." Down the hall my roommate shakes Veronica awake. She doesn't hesitate but comes to my side, sits next to me on the bed and rubs my back. Veronica will get this flu tomorrow and she doesn't care. She rolls the covers back a little and presses her cool palm to my neck. She rubs her fingertips back and forth on the top of my head where the dip in my skull is. I am eased. She is comfort, like my mother's voice. She is safety like the womb I can't remember. She is love like the heartbeat I felt next to my own. She is before we were born.

I need her.

I need her to need me.

The sisters lived in separate cities after they graduated college, but they talked on the phone every day. They were geographically separated but still bound together emotionally. Then came Veronica's decision to move to a remote town in order to pursue a graduate degree. Shaken, yet inspired, by her sister's independent spirit, Megan made an equally radical decision. She took a job in Tokyo. It wasn't long after she settled into her new life that she began a relationship with Paul. These major changes created significant emotional hurdles for both young women.

Megan said that she was deeply concerned about how she would manage without Veronica and how moving so far away would affect their relationship. "Without Veronica there, I had to learn to confide in my new girlfriends and ask them for help in making decisions about my relationship with Paul. That was definitely new for me; I'd never needed anyone else to talk to except Veronica. I also talked to my mom on the phone much more often than I usually had. My mom told me that I should do what I thought would make me happy and not worry about what everyone else thinks, by which she meant not to worry about what Veronica would think. I was still feeling that I might be letting Veronica down if I made a decision to get closer to Paul and live in another country indefinitely. Being so far away from Veronica, it felt as if we were on different planets."

Megan's relationship to Paul began to develop. She loved that he was passionate about the same things she was and that he was both an adventurer and a homebody. She appreciated his sense of humor, warmth, and intelligence and found him to be a wonderful companion. Still, she had difficulty communicating with him. She had a hard time talking to Paul about intimate issues because she expected him to know her in the way that Veronica always had. It surprised her when Paul didn't automatically know what she was feeling. She was taken aback when she had to explain herself in order for him to understand what was going on with her because Veronica "just knew" without their needing to talk things over. Because Megan had no experience communicating on a deep level with anyone other than Veronica, with whom verbal communication was often unnecessary, it was hard for her to get to know Paul deeply. And since Veronica had always known what Megan needed and what she was thinking, Megan now expected Paul to know her in the same way, which of course was impossible. Over the course of several months, however, Megan grew to trust Paul and to be able to open up with him. Now she was nervous about his meeting Veronica, who was coming for a visit. Would Paul and Veronica approve of each other? Would Veronica feel displaced and hurt by Megan's new relationship? Would Paul be intimidated by the sisters' closeness? And might he react strangely to the whole twin thing?

To his credit, Paul didn't ask either sister any annoying twin questions. He was warm and outgoing toward Veronica and teased her in a brotherly way, but he wasn't in the least bit flirtatious. He told Megan, "Veronica's not you—you're so vivacious and fun loving. She doesn't have your glow. I'm attracted to you, not her." Megan was pleased by the compliments, but at the same time she couldn't help feeling defensive on Veronica's behalf. Even Paul's moderate criticism of Veronica hurt Megan, as if she were the one who didn't have the special "glow" Paul had referred to. Still, Megan felt an enormous sense of relief that Veronica didn't feel jealous or hurt by Megan's involvement with Paul. She told Megan that she was genuinely happy that Megan had found someone. Hearing that from Veronica was something that mattered more to Megan than anything else.

Megan decided to remain overseas and give her relationship with Paul a chance. But she told me that she was afraid her decision might forever shift the nature of her relationship with Veronica. She was already worried that, in her absence, Veronica was getting closer to their older sister, which made Megan feel left out and jealous. Still, Megan believed that her ties to Veronica would always remain strong, and she felt ready to separate from her in favor of committing to a love relationship. Megan told me, "I am making the decision to risk being abandoned by Paul rather than choosing the secure position of being close to my sisters and family. If I were to leave now, I would never know whether my relationship with Paul could work out, but I know that my sister will always be there for me."

Throughout their lives, Megan was rarely able to put her own needs ahead of Veronica's, and doing so still caused her to feel conflicted. She still wondered if she was being disloyal to Veronica by being true to herself. I explained to Megan that being attached to a twin sibling is unlike any other relationship, so her sense of feeling conflicted, even though she'd made a reasonable, healthy decision to live apart from Veronica, was completely understandable. Fortunately, Veronica had come to the same conclusion as her sister: that each needed to lead her own life. The last time Megan and I spoke, she said, "I feel so good when Veronica and I talk to each other, and she reassures me that I am making the right decision, that I am following my dream and passion and that I should not feel guilty about being away from my family. When Veronica is supportive and understanding, I miss her even more."

Veronica still wrestled with Megan's absence, and part of her struggle was letting go of the comparison/competition conundrum with which she and Megan grappled for so many years. "If Megan was the good student, I had to be the bad girl in order to prove I was myself and not her. So, now that Megan is happy with her life choices and I'm happy with mine, even though they are so diametrically opposed, I sometimes feel that this means one of us has to be wrong—because how can it be that we are both embracing such different lifestyles and are still happy?" Veronica said she tended to cling to the belief that "if I am right, you are wrong," rather than realizing that two adult women had chosen two different paths. Her challenge was learning to accept that their differences were okay, that comparison and competition didn't need to be the hallmarks of her relationship to her sister, that it was okay for Megan to have a career in another city and a close relationship with Paul—and for her to enjoy her own life apart from Megan.

Veronica came to many realizations in the course of her separation from Megan and credited our initial conversations with opening the door to talks with Megan about their relationship. The sisters had never really discussed certain aspects of being a twin because such subjects seemed taboo. Both Veronica and Megan were surprised to learn that twins would need to talk about problems between them. "Why would best friends have problems?" was their initial take on twinship prior to our conversations. It was liberating for each of them to be able to confront such dilemmas as feeling guilty about having a boyfriend, feeling competitive with your twin when you only want to be accepted for your own strengths, or feeling obliged to be different from your twin in order to prove you're not her. Although they believed their parents had encouraged each of them to pursue their own paths, the twin mystique was also part of the family's belief system. Neither sister experienced being emotionally independent from the other until Megan's move.

Megan and Veronica's story offers a poignant lesson in how difficult it can be for an adult twin to enter into a love relationship without the intense fear that doing so might alienate her same-age sibling. When twins grow up in a family and a culture that buys into the twin mystique, they believe they should be more intimate with each other than with anyone else and that they are each other's soul mate forever. Their experience may bear that out to some degree; yet, it is sadly ironic that twins often withhold some of their most intimate thoughts, especially concerns they have about the twinship, from each other to avoid hurtfulness. Megan's relationship with Paul was an intimate part of her life that she feared discussing with Veronica. Like so many other adult twins, she worried that allowing herself to fall in love might be damaging to her sister.

As parents, how can we help prevent such fears in our adult twins? If we foster a close relationship with each twin throughout their childhood, and if we make sure that each child has the chance to enjoy friendships and experiences apart from the other, then their twin relationship will not take on the overblown significance that the twin mystique engenders. If we want our children to feel free to engage in healthy adult relationships, we need to set them free from the limiting insularity of twin dependence.

For both Megan and Veronica, the challenge now is to believe in their hearts that each is entitled to fall in love and to enjoy an independent, fulfilling life and that doing so is not an offense to the other.

Too Tied to Each Other?

Megan and Veronica's parallel personal histories reached a crossroads where both young women were able to define themselves as individuals and begin to lead lives that each had consciously chosen for herself. Unfortunately, not all sets of twins who were so closely tied as children are able to achieve that level of emotional independence from their same-age sibling. When the parenting principles we've discussed throughout this book have been largely neglected, twins may reach adulthood lacking the self-awareness to know who they are apart from each other.

While they might live in separate cities, as do both sets of twins whose stories you're about to hear, their emotional connectedness prevents them from fully knowing who they are without the other—and from making decisions based on their own needs and desires.

Heather and Faith were twenty-nine-year-old identical twins. Both were accomplished academics who had attended the same prestigious university. Heather became a pharmacist, and Faith worked for a real estate firm. They lived in separate cities within fifty miles of one another. They spoke to each other frequently on the phone and saw one another as often as they could. On the surface, it appeared that these sisters were close, caring, and intimate—and fairly independent.

Having brought the girls up to be nurturing and compassionate toward each other, their mother was proud of the fact that Heather and Faith had never had any real fights or disagreements. She revered their devotion to and concern for one another and appeared to measure her maternal success by her daughters' lack of conflict, selfishness, or volatility. The unfortunate truth, however, was that neither young woman had ever had the opportunity to find out who she was apart from her twin.

When I met with Faith and Heather, I was struck by their rather bland, unexpressive personalities, as if each young woman's individual authenticity had never been allowed to develop. Speaking lovingly about their closeness and describing the other as her best friend, both women said that they hoped to have twins themselves so that they could relive their special relationship. Both acknowledged that they felt terribly upset when the other was unhappy, and they did whatever they could to make sure that didn't happen. Although their conversations with me made it sound as if the two couldn't be more intimately connected, each woman seemed to harbor ambivalent feelings toward the other that they were unable to express. True intimacy includes the capacity to acknowledge and articulate ambivalence, but neither Faith nor Heather could do so.

My sense of these twin sisters was that they didn't develop authentic personalities because they closely followed their mother's guidelines for how twins were supposed to behave and relate to each other. It was as if she had handed them a script that spelled out exactly how they should feel and act. There was no room in her perfect twin script for their individual voices to emerge. Instead, the sisters were supposed to get along happily, always be there for each other, always be the most important person in each other's lives, and make sure that everything was always fair and equal between them.

What gives an individual her own voice? It is her spontaneity, her sense of her own feelings and ideas, her sense of what she wants and what she doesn't want. Having her own voice means that a twin has thoughts and needs and choices that are validated by her parents when she's young and decided upon independently when she's an adult. Heather and Faith rarely had chances to explore their separate feelings, desires, thoughts, and interests without considering how the other would be impacted. They were never separated when they were young. They attended the same high school and the same college. They had the same friends. The only difference in their lives was the sports activities they chose in high school. Heather went out for soccer, and Faith was on the volleyball team. And yet, both stopped those activities at the very same time. Faith was injured and had to quit the team, and so Heather stopped playing soccer.

At twenty-nine, neither Heather nor Faith had ever had a boyfriend. They had never had a fight because fighting wasn't acknowledged by their mother as something that twins do. Fighting might have given each girl the chance to express who she was and how she felt about a particular decision or situation, but it would have upset the twin equilibrium that mom believed was essential. Like other parents whom we've met throughout the book, Heather and Faith's mother was so invested in her daughters' exemplary twin bond that she failed to spend alone time with either girl or to provide either one with sufficient separate experiences that would have helped each discover her unique identity. Twin sisters can be good friends, even best friends, without sacrificing their own individuality. When that authentic sense of self is never allowed to blossom because twins are always being thrown together, treated as an adorable twosome, or left to their own private world, each grows up not knowing how to function as a "me" instead of a "we."

A crucial part of our parental role is to encourage each twin to learn about who she is on her own, just as a singleton would. Bonding with each child as they're growing up, giving each one our individualized attention and guidance, and assuring that each twin has enough opportunities to develop the emotional strength and confidence to make it in the world on her own are our goals. Parents feel overwhelmed when their daughters and sons end up making statements such as these:

> "I've never learned how to exist as an individual."

> "When I'm not with her, I feel half-empty."

> "My longing for her is constant."

"Not to have her by my side one day is inconceivable."

"I put her above everyone, including my boyfriend and parents."

"She is almost-me."

"We live for each other."

Each of these statements was made by a college-educated woman in her early twenties whose story was very similar to Faith and Heather's. She described the semester in graduate school when her sister lived three hundred miles away as torment. And this young woman's inability to achieve emotional independence from her twin is not unusual.

Tony and Frank, twenty-six-year-old twin brothers, were best buddies growing up and lived together all through college and afterwards, until they were twenty-two. It was then that Tony left town all of a sudden with a lover, leaving Frank feeling terribly angry, abandoned, and betrayed. Frank and Tony were both gay, and both subsequently became involved in relationships, but neither felt as close to his lover as to his twin brother. Both brothers had had trouble realizing and accepting that their lovers didn't know what they were thinking the way their twin had always seemed to. "I've had to get used to telling my lover how I feel, what I need, unlike with Frank," Tony said.

The brothers talked online every day and got together three or four times a year, including on their birthday, but had learned that they could not have others around them when they were together—neither their respective partners nor their mother. They needed the exclusive time alone together and couldn't understand why others might feel excluded. Tony called their relationship a partnership. "When we're together," he said, "it's like a light bulb connecting—instant and wonderful." The two had thought about working together but realized that their physical separation was a positive thing, making their time together "more wonderful." Tony felt that their initial "breakup" (his term) when they were twenty-two was good in that it empowered each of them to separate physically. "But I feel bad about putting Frank through such a rough time."

Were there any rough times when the two were children that had to do with being twins? Tony conceded that as a boy he was disappointed when his family couldn't celebrate his achievements, including his being selected as valedictorian of his high school class, for fear that Frank might feel badly. And he wished he had had more privacy growing up. Still, he and Frank talked about their homosexuality together and supported each other as they faced the homophobia of their small-town environment. Frank told me that he and Tony took care of each other as boys. When they were called "sissy" or "fag," each would stand up for the other. Growing up without a father, Frank said, the two brothers "soothed each other through all sorts of traumas. And we also kept each other in line." Frank said that he only wished Tony the best and did not feel badly when good things happened to Tony and not to him, although Tony thought otherwise.

When I mentioned the issue of alone time with their mother (their father had died when the boys were young), both men were resistant to the idea. They remarked that it was counterintuitive to think that separation helps to make twins' relationships healthier. "Even if our mom had had the luxury of help," Frank told me, "she would not have taken us out separately because that was just not part of her thinking."

Frank and Tony's story—as well as Heather and Faith's—point out some of the repercussions when twins have been too closely enmeshed as children. Like Heather and Faith—and the young woman whose statements I quoted earlier—some twins may be so inexperienced at "existing as an individual" that making independent life choices is virtually impossible. If a desired career opportunity means moving a hundred miles away from her sister, a twin may hold herself back from making that choice. Or a twin may be unable to get close to a boyfriend or a husband because she doesn't know how to get to know someone who doesn't already "know her better than she knows herself." Like Tony and Frank, an adult twin may finally be able to enjoy a love relationship only to find himself constantly comparing its deficiencies to "the perfect partnership" he enjoyed with his twin. Or he may not want to get involved with a lover at all because he doesn't want an "outside involvement" to cause a "breakup" of the twinship. Stories abound in the twin literature about a married twin's feeling enormously disappointed that his or her spouse does not live up to the loving, empathic companion that his or her twin epitomized. Many twins are so accustomed to their same-age sibling's anticipating their feelings and needs that a spouse's efforts pale in comparison.

Wishing that their boyfriend, girlfriend, or spouse were more like their twin is, unfortunately, a common refrain. Sometimes, however, twins become involved in a love relationship whose psychological dynamic eerily resembles that of their twinship. Such a scenario is also an unhealthy one.

When a Twin's Love Relationship Mirrors His Too-Close Twinship

Often a twin who has not sufficiently separated from his same-age sibling will duplicate in his love relationship or marriage the behavioral patterns he learned in the twinship. Even when a twin believes that he has achieved independence from his twin, his relationship or marriage may become another twinlike connection that repeats unhealthy aspects of that bond. And he may not even be aware that he is replaying his old twinship role.

If, for example, a twin had always taken care of his same-age sibling, he might fall into that role once again with a mate. In fact, he might unconsciously look for someone with whom he might comfortably replicate that well-known pattern. If the woman he chooses has psychological needs that motivate her to find someone who is a caretaker, the two may function well for a time. But the caretaker/taken-care-of dynamic will likely backfire when one or both partners begin to resent their prescribed roles. Healthy relationships depend on each person's having a developed sense of self. When one lacks an identity beyond that of a caretaker and when the other cannot function comfortably without her partner seeing to her every need, neither individual feels truly happy or fulfilled.

Philip and Nicole were twenty-seven-year-old fraternal twins. Philip might qualify as the fantasy big brother every young girl dreams of: protective, caring, a strong shoulder to cry on, a good-natured, savvy guy friend to hang out with and show you the ropes. Except that Philip was not Nicole's older brother; he was her twin brother. But he always treated Nicole like his younger sister. He was her protector, and she was his nearly constant companion whom he took pride in protecting. "Nicole probably wouldn't have had the nerve to do half the stuff I made her try as a teenager if I hadn't pushed her," Philip told me. "I took her horseback riding on this rocky beach in Mexico one time, even though she told me she was afraid of horses. 'How can you be afraid if I'm gonna be riding right next to you,' I told her—and I was right. She faced her fear because she knew I'd never let anything happen to her."

Horseback riding wasn't the only instance when Nicole required Philip's emotional support. She was shy as a child and found it easier to be with Philip's friends than to make her own. "I almost always included her when I'd go out with my friends, even when we got to high school," Philip said. There were times, however, when Nicole wasn't included—when Philip began dating in his late teens. "She never said she was jealous, but I remember coming home one night and going into her room to tell her about a girl I'd gone out with. I really liked this particular girl—she was smart and cute and had a great sense of humor—but while I was telling Nicole about her, I could see something change in her expression. She pretended to be happy for me, but I could tell she felt really sad."

Philip and Nicole went to separate colleges but kept in close touch through daily e-mails and phone calls. This wasn't enough for Nicole, who had a very tough time separating from her brother. Like many twins who have never separated before, then are forced to do so abruptly, Nicole felt utterly desolate, abandoned, and grief stricken—almost as if she had suffered a death. Philip tried to talk her through it, convince her as he always had that she'd be fine and that he was still there for her, but this time he wasn't physically around to help Nicole deal with her fears. Luckily, her roommate suggested that Nicole seek therapy, and Nicole managed to find a therapist who was knowledgeable in twinship issues. Nicole began to work through her dependence on Philip and to understand why it had taken root so early in their childhood. She made progress with her therapy, made a few friends, and actually began to create a separate life for herself at college. But her near breakdown took its toll on Philip. "I was a wreck that year," he told me. "It seemed like Nicole was constantly calling or contacting me. And I felt so helpless—and tapped out. I guess a part of me felt angry, too, but I couldn't admit that then. I felt too guilty."

Almost eight years later, in his last year of medical school, Philip met someone he was serious about. They shared a lot of the same interests, and Philip felt powerfully attracted to her. But there were problems. "I thought I really loved this woman, even considered asking her to marry me," Philip said. "But after about three months, I noticed there was something about her that had that twinge of helplessness. Like she was depending on me too much. She had a good job, but she hinted that she would love to have a less stressful life. I got the idea that if we got married, she might want to stop working. I felt weird about that."

Philip had fallen into a common pattern that adult twins often experience. He had chosen a partner with whom he repeated the emotional dynamic he'd had with Nicole. Perhaps this woman's dependency had initially attracted him; certainly it would have felt familiar. But Philip was aware enough to sense that he didn't want to go there again. He had finally gained his independence from Nicole and didn't want to have to replay the role that had defined him for his entire childhood. Until he broke free from it, he couldn't ever develop into the kind of man he wanted to become. He would never be free to make choices based on what he truly wanted and needed if he remained tied to his old twinship pattern of being the protector for someone who needed protecting.

Philip came to realize that he'd rather be in a relationship with someone who was more his equal, "someone I don't have to constantly worry about or take care of." As familiar as the role of protector felt for him, he said he was finally ready to give it up. As a positive consequence of Nicole's near breakdown during her first year of college, she was able to talk to Philip about their relationship and how it had been detrimental to both of them in many ways. So, by the time his affair with the woman he almost married was breaking up, Philip understood how it related to his twinship with Nicole. And he knew he would choose differently next time.

Same-sex twins might just as easily confront the scenario Philip faced with his girlfriend: falling into a relationship that seems to mirror what they went through with their twin. There's a longing, often unacknowledged, to replace the intimacy that they might have had with their twin, and getting involved with someone they can play that old role with can feel comfortable. On the other hand, sometimes a twin might opt for the exact opposite dynamic as what he experienced with his same-age sibling. If, for example, a twin had been the passive one, he might finally want to feel as if he is in charge, thus becoming involved with someone whom he can take care of or even dominate. The point is, as long as a twin is making choices based on prescribed patterns related to the twinship, rather than conscious choices that emanate from a fully individualized self, that person remains stuck in the past.

Nicole was wise to seek therapy when she did, and Philip benefited from the subsequent talks they had about their childhood relationship. It comes as no surprise that their upbringing had not included the principles we have discussed throughout this book. Fortunately, both Nicole and Philip committed to learning who they were as individuals and to making choices based on what was best for each of them as separate people.

Can Adult Twins Break Free from Unhealthy Patterns?

In the early years of my marriage, I had little awareness that my ongoing behavior toward my sister served to perpetuate the childhood roles we each had played. I had been the caregiver, and she had been the recipient of the caregiving. We were both so locked into our assigned parts that, as adults, neither Jane nor I were familiar with those aspects of each other's personality that fell outside our set pattern of interacting. We were stuck in our old ways of relating and, sadly, were missing out on actually getting to know who each of us was beyond the roles we had always played as twins.

When my husband would mention that my behavior toward Jane often seemed tinged with envy, hostility, or secrecy, I would brush his comments off as either unimportant or mysterious—something he couldn't possibly comprehend as a nontwin. To my dismay, many of his observations were valid. Back then, though, I would find a way to excuse or rationalize Jane's and my behavior toward each other as a means of protecting our twinship. Although I knew intellectually that our relationship could withstand a major blowup, I acted as if I was bound to honor a sacred bond. And this bond kept me from confronting my sister about how we treated each other. I was afraid of losing her and inexperienced at treating her like the individual she was.

For me, two major influences allowed for a positive shift in my relationship with Jane: therapy and getting married. In therapy, I was finally able to confront issues that had always been uncomfortable for me to talk about, including the false expectation that Jane and I were supposed to be intensely close just because we were twins, the competition and jealousy between us, and the guilt I felt when things went well for me and not for Jane.

I also came to realize that Jane and I didn't really know each other beyond the roles we had played as twins. I had always assumed, for example, that she felt everything I was feeling, which was not true at all. And why should it be? She is not me; she is Jane.

Getting married helped me to understand my relationship with Jane in that I discovered my own capacity to be truly intimate. Jane and I had shared a sisterly closeness, but we had never been able to be truly honest or vulnerable with each other. Having my own separate adult life finally allowed me to have separate experiences and to affirm the fact that those experiences wouldn't disrupt the twinship. Jane and I could still be close friends even though I now had someone in my life with whom I had a stronger attachment.

As I came to understand that a childhood connection is different from an adult connection, I realized that my relationship with Jane had to be redefined. Adults are more capable of self-reflection, more able to articulate their own experiences, more capable of taking responsibility for their feelings and actions, and more perceptive about themselves and others. And all of these skills require an increasing sense of self-confidence and self-awareness. Young adults who aren't twins have a tough enough time with all of this, and for twins the challenge is considerably greater. For twins who grew up with an unhealthy, enmeshed connection, like Jane and me, developing those skills is more daunting still.

For me, a defining moment came when I realized that, in the interest of becoming my own person, it was okay to put myself first. In fact, it was alright to be "self-ish."

It's Okay for a
Twin to Be Self-ish

If I could sum up the advice a parent might give to his adult twin who is still struggling to be his own person, it would be this: it's okay and necessary to focus on yourself and your needs because doing so will help you discover who you are apart from your twin. Everyone deserves to know who he is and to develop fully as an individual.

When an adult twin has her own sense of self, she is motivated by what she wants and needs and feels, and she makes decisions based on those needs and desires. This is not to say that she disregards others. But for twins who are so often plagued by the need to consider their same-age sibling, it is a powerful lesson to learn to act on your own behalf. When you are able to live your life according to who you are, your life becomes authentically your own. You may continue to wonder how what you do affects your twin, but you will be much less burdened by the emotional weight of an intractable twinship. Instead, you'll be able to follow your own path without concern that every step you take will have a direct and altering impact on your twin sibling. You will feel the freedom of creating your own personal map.

I think that's what Megan learned. Having a boyfriend, moving to another city, enjoying herself apart from her twin sister— these things made her feel guilty and self-involved at first because in the back of her mind, she kept wondering and worrying about Veronica. Megan needed the physical distance to ease her way into creating the emotional distance from someone she loved but finally needed to separate from.

It is essential and healthy for young-adult twins to lead separate lives, whether they live on the same block or thousands of miles apart. The separateness allows them to make space for their own sense of self and for their discovery of relationships other than the twinship. A twin may feel self-centered when she thinks of herself first, when she has a singular dream and begins to pursue it. But being "self-ish" in this way is exactly what a twin needs to do in order to pursue a fulfilling life as an individual.

Having separate careers, interests, and friends means that each twin will have a lot going on in their lives aside from their relationship to each other. It does not mean twins won't love each other or be there for each other or share a uniquely close connection. Jane and I certainly do.

Parents-of-Twins Journal: Young Adults

WRITE DOWN YOUR THOUGHTS

If your twins have not yet reached young adulthood:

- How do you envision your twins' relationship when they're grown up?
- In what ways do you anticipate that their life choices will be influenced by their twinship?
- In what ways do you think your parenting philosophy and strategies ensure that your twins will enjoy both a close friendship and authentically independent lives?

If your twins are now young adults:

- How would you describe your twins' current relationship to each other?

- How do you think their current relationship reflects how your twins related to each other as children?
- In what ways do you think each twin has been affected by being a twin?

Tips for Parents of Young-Adult Twins

- Help your adult twins better understand their twinship by openly responding to questions they might have about their childhood.
- Appreciate each twin for his or her distinct qualities, strengths, and achievements. Avoid comparing your adult twins.
- Don't feel guilty about having different feelings toward each of your adult children—or for worrying about one's weaknesses more than the other's.
- If you think that one or both of your twins might be struggling with issues relating to the twinship, suggest that counseling would be a safe way to talk about these problems or concerns.
- Don't ask one twin to report to you about what's going on in the other's life. If you're concerned about one twin, go to the source and communicate with him or her directly.
- Continue to spend alone time with each young adult and get to know the person each has become.

Resource Guide

Center for Loss in Multiple Birth (CLIMB)
P.O. Box 91377
Anchorage, AK 99509
(907) 222-5321
www.climbsupport.org

The Center for the Study of Multiple Birth (CSMB)
333 E. Superior St., Ste. 464
Chicago, IL 60611
(312) 695-1677
www.multiplebirth.com

Fetal Hope Foundation
9786 South Holland St.
Littleton, CO 80127
(877) 789-HOPE
www.fetalhope.org

International Society for Twin Studies (ISTS)
Queensland Institute of Medical Research,
Post Office Royal Brisbane Hospital
Brisbane, QLD 4029, Australia
www.ists.qimr.edu.au

International Twins Association
6898 Channel Rd., N.E.
Minneapolis, MN 55432
(612) 571-3022
www.intltwins.org

National Organization of Mothers of Twins Clubs, Inc. (NOMOTC)
P.O. Box 700860
Plymouth, MI 48170
(877) 540-2200
www.nomotc.org

Twinless Twins Support Group
P.O. Box 980481
Ypsilanti, MI 48198
(888) 205-8962
www.twinlesstwins.org

**Twins and Multiple Births
Association (TAMBA)
(United Kingdom)**
2 The Willows
Gardner Road
Guildford, Surrey,
England
GU1 4PG
(011) (44) 870-770-3305
www.tamba.org.uk

The Twins Foundation
P.O. Box 6043
Providence, RI 02940
(401) 751-TWIN
www.twinsfoundation.com

Twins Magazine
11211 E. Arapahoe Rd., Ste. 101
Centennial, CO 80112
(888) 55-TWINS
www.twinsmagazine.com

Two, Four, Six, Eight
Web site for Educating Multiples
www.twinsandmultiples.org

Acknowledgments

I am deeply grateful to my loving "singleton" children, Matthew, Sarah, and Amy, who would often note how challenging it is to be a sibling to twins but who were remarkable in their patient willingness to help my husband, Robert, and me negotiate our very busy household, and even more remarkable in the recognition and appreciation that they gave to their younger twin brothers as two distinct individuals. My twin sons, Jonny and David, have contributed endlessly to my insight about what it means to be a twin. I delight in their unique loving selves and enjoy how much they enrich each other's lives without malice or intrusion.

My relationship with my twin sister, Jane, has been an incomparable aspect of who I am. Laughing together and appreciating life events from our special perspective as twins is such a pleasure and a gift. Both of us truly treasure our twinship because we have worked so diligently to express and maintain our individuality.

My gratitude, appreciation, and love belong to Dr. Estelle Shane. She has been my mentor, girlfriend, colleague, and surrogate mother for many years. Her belief in my ideas and intellectual gifts helped me realize my dream of writing a book about twin development.

Dr. Nancy Gordon Seif has been my best friend since we met on the very first day of our college freshman orientation. She mirrored my strengths and talents even before I could access them. Talking with Nancy, who is now my colleague as well, about all aspects of this book has been invaluable, including her editorial direction.

I am eternally grateful for my psychoanalytic training at the Institute for Contemporary Psychoanalysis in Los Angeles. My affiliation has enabled me to feel comfortable about sharing renegade ideas within a receptive and supportive environment.

I cannot say enough about the many mothers and fathers of twins whom I have come to know intimately over the course of numerous years. As I shared with them my knowledge of twinship issues and my philosophical beliefs about how to raise emotionally healthy twins, I, too, learned so much from the experiences and concerns that they shared with me.

What good fortune to have worked with writer Laura Golden Bellotti. She and I share healthy "twinlike" qualities that made our collaboration extraordinary and rewarding.

Many thanks to my gracious editors, Marnie Cochran and Renee Sedliar, whose enthusiasm and encouragement have been essential to the creation of this book.

Of course, I want to thank my agent, Ellen Geiger, whose good counsel I value and who found a terrific home for this book at Da Capo Press.

I would like to pay tribute to my dear friend Dr. Michael Mc-Grail who, so sadly, did not live to see this book published. He was a constant source of good humor and moral support throughout the writing process.

Finally, I thank my husband, Robert, for his love, support, tenacity, and strength. His optimism and boundless joy in living have had a profound impact on me and our family. He has inspired all of us to be expansive and daring in countless ways. Forever invested in our growth and development, he ensures that opportunities and adventures abound.

Index